Leah companions us as a friend leading us through educating our children, loving them well, drawing recognizing their potential. This book will gently e exactly the mother your children need. Then she equips us to move forward with confidence. Highly recommended.

SALLY CLARKSON, author of many inspiring books, including *Awaking Wonder,* and host of the podcast *At Home with Sally*

The friend and mentor that you have always wanted at your side as you educate your children, Leah's book will speak life into your home learning. Both encouraging you and giving you the practical tools that you need to bring a Charlotte Mason–inspired education to your own home, Leah reveals the remarkable wisdom and philosophy of a Charlotte Mason education. This book truly is the *For the Children's Sake* of our time.

LYNN SEDDON, founder of Raising Little Shoots

What a joy it is to remember that children are born persons, that a little masterly inactivity creates space for learning, and that a feast of ideas is the true animating force of education. I wanted to linger on these pages remembering my children's homeschool journey with Charlotte Mason as a guide. In this timely new book, Charlotte is revealed as a whole person whose ideas are here to stay—ideas validated by a century of research since! *Modern Miss Mason* is the Charlotte Mason book for our era. Boden captures both the essence of Charlotte's revolutionary approach to education while liberating her from ideological hot takes that leave parents overwhelmed and self-critical. Written with a lyrical voice, sharing a wide array of fascinating examples and personal experiences, Boden offers the weary parent and home educator a cozy nook to relax, reflect, and recharge with Charlotte's comforting voice to guide us.

JULIE BOGART, author of *The Brave Learner* and founder of BraveWriter.com

Modern Miss Mason is a beautiful call to freedom in our literature-based homeschool. Leah Boden offers inspiration to take the life-giving philosophy of Charlotte Mason and adapt it to our own interests and callings, so that instead of being bound by a rigid framework, we are given the tools to lay a feast of learning. In *Modern Miss Mason*, Leah helps us curate an education for our children that will empower them to be lifelong learners and will bring us joy in the process.

JENNIFER PEPITO, author of *Mothering by the Book*

Leah is a wise mentor and gentle guide who leads her reader into a way of engaging with education that is also a real immersion in wonder, imagination, and joy. Her work here is a gift as she offers a way of learning and education that will craft rich, rooted souls.

SARAH CLARKSON, author of *This Beautiful Truth* and *Book Girl*

Like a breath of fresh air! Free of the usual "musts" and "shoulds," Leah Boden lovingly invites us to the Charlotte Mason philosophy, an education and life where everyone is welcome.

DR. GEMMA ELIZABETH, writer and podcaster, *Our Muslim Homeschool*

Leah invites us all to become modern Miss Masons, and I've never felt more inspired to do so. She seamlessly weaves the inherent freedom of a living education into each chapter while describing the inner workings of a lifegiving home. I feel seen, known, and valued as Leah expands the bounds of tradition to embrace Charlotte Mason's principles within the context of today's vibrant family life.

AMBER O'NEAL JOHNSTON, author of *A Place to Belong: Celebrating Diversity and Kinship in the Home and Beyond*

Modern Miss Mason breathed excitement and inspiration into me while simultaneously enveloping me in peaceful confidence. In her own beautiful way, Leah showed me how Charlotte Mason's ideals could have a profound effect on my children, their education, and my mothering. My only wish is that I could have had this book at the very start of my motherhood journey! *Modern Miss Mason* is a gift that will impact whole families for many years to come.

GRETA ESKRIDGE, author of *Adventuring Together: How to Create Connections and Make Lasting Memories with Your Kids* and *100 Days of Adventure: Nature Activities, Creative Projects, and Field Trips for Every Season*

Leah Boden's lovely book and lovely life embody all that Charlotte Mason stood for over 100 years ago. Her deep understanding of Charlotte's principles and her commonsense approach to real children make this book just the new vision we have needed to continue passing these ideas to generations to come.

CINDY ROLLINS, Morningtimeformoms.com

Modern Miss Mason

Discover How Charlotte Mason's
Revolutionary Ideas on Home Education
Can Change How You & Your Children
Learn & Grow Together

LEAH BODEN

TYNDALE
MOMENTUM®

A Tyndale nonfiction imprint

Visit Tyndale online at tyndale.com.

Visit Tyndale Momentum online at tyndalemomentum.com.

Visit the author online at leahboden.com.

Tyndale, Tyndale's quill logo, *Tyndale Momentum*, and the Tyndale Momentum logo are registered trademarks of Tyndale House Ministries. Tyndale Momentum is a nonfiction imprint of Tyndale House Publishers, Carol Stream, Illinois.

Designed by Libby Dykstra

Edited by Deborah King

Published in association with the literary agency of Punchline Agency LLC.

For information about special discounts for bulk purchases, please contact Tyndale House Publishers at csresponse@tyndale.com, or call 1-855-277-9400.

Library of Congress Cataloging-in-Publication Data

A catalog record for this book is available from the Library of Congress.

ISBN 978-1-4964-5852-0

Printed in the United States of America

28 27 26 25 24 23
7   6   5   4   3

This book is dedicated to my husband, Dave, who voluntarily entered my world and sought to find his own understanding of Charlotte Mason's work in support of mine.

Also, to my children: Nyah, Joel, Micah, and Sienna-Raine, who have patiently pioneered Charlotte's educational ideas alongside me.

Contents

A Note to the Reader

I've never been one for titles, either being given one or using them for others. (There are, of course, exceptions; anyone who has worked tirelessly for a PhD gets "Doc" from me, whether they like it or not.) However, I am an advocate of honour being given where honour is due. I suspect the two hundred pages of words you're about to read give Charlotte Maria Shaw Mason the absolute credit and dignity she deserves, so I also think you'll forgive my impertinence for referring to her as "Charlotte" throughout this book!

Modern Miss Mason isn't an academic paper, so I wanted to avoid applying the much-used "Mason" as her title throughout my writing. And as beloved as the name is, I also wanted to avoid focusing too much on her marital status by referring to her continuously as "Miss Mason." Charlotte has become a friend, a true mentor, someone whose work and words have walked alongside my mothering and educating journey for many years. So, there we have it: Charlotte.

And though she be but little, she is fierce.
SHAKESPEARE, *A Midsummer Night's Dream*

Foreword

I had never heard of Charlotte Mason when I started homeschooling twelve years ago. I was only familiar with the big box curriculums and reading regimens I assumed all good homeschoolers used.

But it soon became apparent that homeschooling and I were never going to make it if something didn't change. I needed our daily practices to align with the values of my heart.

I knew that reading great literature with my children created meaningful connection and opened the door for incredible conversations. I knew that giving them plenty of time in nature awakened their senses and opened a whole new world of discovery and exploration. And I knew that play was a masterful way of learning, that late is better than too early, and that childhood was worth preserving.

I also knew that I couldn't stick to a curriculum to save my life.

The books were wonderful, but everything else felt too scripted. I found myself coming up with creative lessons on the fly each day, despite the huge investment I had made in all those resources.

But then one beautiful fall day, I was sitting in the backyard talking to my friend Stephanie on the phone. My kids were building a teepee out of branches, and I was relishing the freedom this lifestyle offered us.

I told Stephanie about our recent adventures and favorite activities together, which included nature journaling, handcrafting, and visiting museums. I confided to her that I was skipping the worksheets and textbooks.

She said, "You're so Charlotte Mason."

I had no idea what she meant by that, but I jotted down the name to research later. When I did, I was forever changed by what—or shall I say *who*—I discovered.

Charlotte's writings embodied everything I believed in my heart about education but had not been able to articulate. Her insight into childhood affirmed everything I had sensed when I observed my kids. She was able to see that children need wonder and "a quiet growing time" all while holding the capacity for a rich thought life and for grasping meaning from books and experiences.

From that day forward, Charlotte, my children, and I set out upon a journey together. We devoured living books, took our nature journaling supplies to local parks, and spent countless hours in nature, allowing curiosity to be our guide. She not only gave me permission to nurture childhood, but she also empowered me to follow my mothering instincts.

In fact, it was Charlotte who inspired a whole movement I started called Wild + Free. Through my work with this beautiful homeschool community, I met Leah Boden.

My friendship with Leah came about, as many relationships do in these modern times, on social media. I was captivated by this lovely English woman living out the principles of an early twentieth-century Charlotte Mason education in the twenty-first century from her own home in Coventry. Her book-lined school cabin tucked behind her house became famous in online communities such as Wild + Free.

And we followed her to her new home by a park where she takes her morning walk every day and regales us with stories of the seasons and sounds of birds in her iconic British accent.

Leah once captivated over a thousand ladies at our Wild + Free conference in Franklin, Tennessee, by reading a passage from *The Secret Garden* in its original Yorkshire dialect. Her inspiring presentation left us speechless and had us all clamoring to return home to read the book aloud to our children once more.

Leah seeks to live an authentic life, to be a student of life, and she follows Charlotte's advice to "do for herself as she would do for her children." She fosters her own growth and knowledge as she seeks to encourage her children to do the same.

I often receive messages from Leah when she visits the Lake District where Charlotte Mason once lived and where Beatrix Potter imagined the world of Peter Rabbit. Leah has read Charlotte's original texts in Ambleside where William Wordsworth once worked and where Charlotte established her House of Education.

This book could just as easily be called *Leah of the Lake District*.

Although Charlotte Mason greatly honored motherhood and offered many an exhortation for mothers throughout her texts, she did not have any children of her own. Leah, unlike Charlotte, is a mother. She understands the great challenge that is being both parent and educator.

Leah is truly a modern Miss Mason because she understands how to integrate Charlotte's principles into our messy, modern-day mothering life. She knows how to balance the ideals of Charlotte's methods within the realities of our complex twenty-first century world.

Leah believes, much like Charlotte did over a hundred years ago, that our job is to cultivate an environment in which our children thrive. To create the kind of homeschools our children need, not the ones in our heads.

It's not easy to homeschool in a society that assesses the merits of education based on the volume of information accumulated, which is precisely what makes Charlotte Mason a true renegade. When I read her works, I find the principles inside aren't antiquated ideas we hope to apply today but rather they are ahead of her time. Perhaps they even transcend time.

You see, people have and always will seek to measure, assess, and put children in a box. We like things neat and tidy, predictable, controllable. But children's minds, hearts, and souls are anything but orderly. They are wild and full of wonder. Curious and full of questions. Passionate and full of possibilities.

If there is one thing children teach us, it is that learning is not linear, and the building blocks of education are not facts and figures but knowledge and ideas.

While several homeschooling pioneers in the US have shed light on the beauty of a Charlotte Mason education over the past thirty years, I believe the modern Miss Mason herself is here for such a time as this.

There is something uniquely compelling about Leah Boden's relationship with Charlotte Mason as an educator in the UK and the fresh perspective she offers us as we endeavor to honor childhood, education, and motherhood in the midst of modern culture. Leah's understanding of Miss Mason's words and ways is a beautiful, ever-growing, ever-evolving work in and of itself. But it is transforming the way home educators experience the joy, awe, and wonder of learning.

Hers is a voice for our generation.

Hers is a message for the world.

Ainsley Arment
Founder of Wild + Free

Walking with Charlotte

*It may be that the souls of all children are waiting for
the call of knowledge to awaken them to delightful living.*
CHARLOTTE MASON, *A PHILOSOPHY OF EDUCATION*

It's 1:50 on a Tuesday afternoon, and the remains of the morning are
sprawled across the schoolroom table: books piled up, a scattering of
coloured pencils, a couple of notebooks, and an art gallery postcard of
Walter Langley's *Never Morning Wore to Evening but Some Heart Did
Break*. Even after over fifteen years of homeschooling and four children, we still haven't perfected this tidying-up-after-lessons thing. My
younger two children have helped themselves to lunch, I'm brewing
my fourth cup of tea of the day, and I quickly check my appearance in
the mirror as I'm about to go on a video call!

At 2 p.m. I have a coaching call with Holly from Ohio. We've never
met before, but I know from her questionnaire that she has three children under nine, she's been homeschooling for four years, she's halfway
through reading Charlotte Mason's first volume *Home Education*, and
pre-children she was a history teacher. We've agreed on some talking
points before we get on the call. I press start on the Zoom call, and her
name appears in the waiting room; I take a deep breath and check that

my hair doesn't look too scary and that the angle of the camera masks the morning's destruction of our learning space.

Our faces appear on the screen, and I smile my biggest smile to welcome her into this strange digital space. Then I raise my mug of tea to show it's all quite relaxed here and say, "Holly, it is so lovely to meet you. How are you doing?" We exchange pleasantries and begin by working through her preconversation questionnaire before we settle into what she really came for.

"So, Holly, tell me about your homeschooling. What are you doing well?"

Silence.

Holly's eyes are big, and I can see a slight panic on her face as she wasn't expecting this question.

I give her time and tell her it's okay, and she eventually says, "Well, I don't know. I guess I'm good at reading aloud to my children. We love our daily walks around the local park, I'm slowly figuring out the best places to buy living books, and I'm finally getting to share my love of history with my children, and they're not bored!"

We laugh, and I respond, "It sounds like you're doing a really good job."

I see the tears fill up in her eyes. No one has told her that in four years.

In her book *Dare to Lead,* sociologist and author Brené Brown states, "I know my life is better when I work from the assumption that everyone is doing the best they can."[1] I've tried to view every woman who comes to me to learn more about homeschooling and Charlotte Mason through this lens. When I speak to them with kindness and understanding, I see them begin to grow and develop in amazing ways. Between the lines of every questionnaire I've read, in the undertones of every conversation I've conducted, the plea is the same.

Every mother is calling out for confidence.

From Humble Beginnings

I was never the girl who picked her baby names by the age of thirteen, dreamed of motherhood, planned to homeschool, or who had a four-ring binder full of magazine articles in readiness for the perfect wedding. I walked the era of teenage heartache and angst but quickly learnt at a young age to hold life lightly, with gratitude and with great intention. After graduating with a somewhat disappointing degree classification (which you'll read about in chapter 10), I set sail for the Americas (or rather, jumped on a plane to St. Louis—but that sounds much less romantic). There, I embarked on a yearlong faith-based programme equipping me in leadership, preaching, campus ministry, and a myriad of other skills that I'm sure I've used here and there over the years. I wiped the floor with my whole cohort in the "Preach-off," and as much as that triumph rates very highly in my memories of my year in Missouri, little did I know that a seed would be sown there that would change my life forever.

It was probably on a Friday, because great things happen on Fridays; they were serving sloppy joes in the associated daycare cafeteria, and my friend Pam and I headed down there to grab lunch. Pam was on staff, was from St. Louis, and had the most beautiful red hair that you had ever seen. She knew everyone, knew what was going on, and most importantly, knew what sloppy joes were!

As we headed to the small kitchen area, a group of older-looking children (older than the daycare children) were milling around in the corridor. Pam knew them and stopped to chat.

"Hey guys, what's up? This is my friend Leah. She's from England."

One of the girls looked me right in the eye, smiled, and replied, "Hello, Miss Leah, pleased to meet you. How are you enjoying your time in St. Louis?"

I kind of stuttered my reply, as I'd never been addressed by a child in this way before. Pam went on to talk to them about a book they were reading; they discussed mutual friends, passed on their regards to each other's parents, and were on their way.

As Pam and I sat down on plastic chairs at the white, metal-legged banqueting tables to a feast of ground beef on bread, I said, "So, who were those children and how do I get one?"

Pam replied, "They're homeschooled but come here to DaySpring a couple of days a week to take subjects they may not do at home."

To which I replied, "They're what?"

For the remaining time left in our lunch break, whilst I was sipping iced water and wishing there was something else for lunch, Pam told me about homeschooling. I was wide eyed and ready to learn, not quite realising that five years later as a wife and new mother to our baby daughter Nyah, I would return to that conversation.

I never ate sloppy joes again.

Remembering St. Louis

Fast-forward to the early 2000s. I had two children at this point, and my friends and I were discussing baby clothes and wooden toys. Then we got onto the topic of school places. Whenever we discussed this, I couldn't shake the conversation Pam and I had in the cafeteria that day, and moreover, the impact the children had on me. I'd bat the thought of it off frequently like an annoying fly, as my husband Dave and I hadn't even discussed it, nor did I know anyone who had embarked on homeschooling in England.

Nyah was given a spot in the local primary school, and with that niggling itch of "something isn't quite right," I went about preparing her to start. I'd begun reading blogs about homeschooling; one of our friends had started by now, and my curiosity was growing. The day came for Nyah to start pre-school. She was dressed in a little grey skirt, a white polo shirt, and a red jumper embroidered with the school logo. The school was not even a five-minute walk from our home, so with her empty red book bag in one hand and my hand gently holding the other one, we set off together to embark on her new adventure. I wasn't teary, I wasn't anxious; Nyah even had a skip in her step, and we chatted as we walked, but I knew, I just knew I didn't want to do this.

In Comes Charlotte

I had so many tabs open on our green Dell laptop that I was sure I was about to cause system overload. I had searched everything from "Is homeschooling legal?" through to "Do homeschooled kids get into university?" I was pregnant with our third child, and between playing Mozart to him in the womb and emailing Dave links to a slew of blog posts about why we should homeschool, I was ravenously reading everything I could get my hands on about teaching my children at home.

Somewhere between the Post-it Notes, computer tabs, folded pages in books, and conversations with friends (who were now homeschooling), I was introduced to Charlotte Mason.

From my first reading about her, I loved how my early (blog) teachers portrayed Charlotte's take on life and education. These simple articles revealed Charlotte's holistic view of children, her freeing methods of finding and applying knowledge, and the vital place of parents in their learning journey. All my hope for my own children's childhoods to be filled with good literature, nature, beauty, and truth was staring at me from blogspot.com! I knew straight away I'd found a suitable travel companion.

We wanted the opportunity to home educate to give our children the chance to learn according to their own stage, not necessarily their age. We wanted to explore a world of learning without standardised testing, star chart reward systems, or classroom seating plans. We wanted to offer our children a wide and varied curriculum of subjects; for them to be able to have the time and space to explore their interests, grow slowly, and discover who they are in their own precious time.

We knew homeschooling would be a sacrifice—financially and time wise—but after many months of work, we were all in!

With Dave and me fully convinced, one million articles on homeschooling read, decisions made, and family told, Nyah wrapped up her one year's experience in school and we then set out on the adventure of a lifetime. The Boden Academy began!

Why Charlotte Mason?

Charlotte Mason's work and words matter. They mattered then, in the early twentieth century when she was moving and shaking ideas up in a stiff Victorian culture, and they matter now as we are submerged in a digital age which is distracting and diverging our attention from the past and quickly deeming old educational ideas out of date or irrelevant.

Charlotte breathed life and wonder back into childhood, and she opened the eyes of parent-teachers and the hearts of students.

Orphaned at seventeen, Charlotte found herself having to forge a path alone. Already experienced in self-education, she had her sights set on teaching, and with the help of supportive adults in her life she continued her journey of working and training to teach children. The Victorian classrooms of England appeared broken to Charlotte; children were raised to work down mines in coal pits and in factories rather than receiving education for life and delight. Charlotte was saddened to see this. She began to write about her findings, hold lectures about her research, and over time gathered a following of parents, teachers, and educational leaders intrigued by her idea of a "living education."

This revolutionary educator, who at the turn of the twentieth century was brave enough to push beyond the norms of educational and societal boundaries, made her mark as a leader in a time when women's voices in society were only just beginning to be heard.

Charlotte built a legacy that still manifests itself in homes and schoolrooms all over the world today. She was an author, speaker, and businesswoman; a teacher and a friend to many; but most of all, she was a faithful advocate for children—and she did all that she did for their sake.

I formed my own timeless bond with Charlotte whilst reading about her life and work. There was something about her approach that reminded me of my 1970s schooling in Pudsey, Leeds. It invoked memories of my childhood connections with nature tables, reading corners, and the freedom to explore outdoors. My initial explorations led me to mostly American websites, complex prescriptive curriculums, seemingly random things tagged with the words *Charlotte Mason*, and books packed with Victorian illustrations. I gleaned as much as I could whilst being slightly baffled that I couldn't find many British followers of this revolutionary British educator (we all found each other eventually). I decided that I would need to go back to the source to truly understand how to move her concepts from page to practice.

Before I knew it, Charlotte's six pink books on education lined my shelves and sat in my lap day after day. These original volumes have formed the foundation of my pedagogy ever since. Our family started slowly resting in a rhythm of nature observation, reading living books, and loving and telling back our tales of poetry, fables, and heroes. We filled pages with pictures of our history adventures; we scoured maps, recited verses, and copied out our favourite lines from our favourite lives. We didn't tick boxes, fill in paperwork, answer rows of questions, or prove what we knew, but instead began to feel alive in our learning together. It was not and still is not a perfect picture. I have come to realise there is no guarantee or magic formula for success, but I feel like we have found a framework for person-centred learning that works even in our modern world.

A Warm Welcome for All

Charlotte Mason designed her ideas to inspire an education for all. This means whatever your family circumstances, whatever the unique and complex needs of your children, and whatever your faith background is, you are welcome here. This is for you. Though she often addresses her advice to parents as a couple (as you will see in this book), I know single homeschooling mums and dads will benefit greatly from it as well.

Woven throughout Charlotte's words are the clear convictions of her faith and Christian practices. Whilst I share Charlotte's faith in Jesus Christ, my expression and experience of the Christian life looks quite different from hers. I didn't come to this pedagogy due to it being a *Christian* education; I was drawn to it because of the freedom I saw for a child's development, and I just so happen to also be a Christian.

Back in 1893, Charlotte visited the Spanish Chapel in Florence, Italy. On the wall of the chapel was a painting with the title *The Triumph of Saint Thomas Aquinas*.[2] The image in the painting is often interpreted as showing the Spirit of God hovering above a myriad of great painters, philosophers, teachers, and educators, inspiring and guiding them to creatively express who they are and bring their contribution to the world. Charlotte wrote about this illustration, saying it depicted the *great recognition* that every educator is destined to make— namely, the recognition that at the deepest source of origin, God is the helper and educator of all mankind and the source of all creative expression. As a Christian, this idea is deeply meaningful to me—but I don't think it is meant to be a barrier for those who don't share my faith. Rather, it is a generous invitation for all to engage with the beauty of education—whether you have a religious background or not.

Like Charlotte, my faith is the cornerstone of my life, and therefore it cannot help but influence every practical, emotional, and relational thread that weaves through our family culture. But we have ultimately established rhythms around faith and practice based on our own biblical convictions, not just the teachings of an educationalist. Whilst we can have heroes and inspirational figures pointing us to truth and freedom, we must go to the source of our own faith to find hope in our home. For me that ultimate person is not Charlotte but rather Jesus Christ. You get to decide who that will be for you.

It's important to me that anyone can come to *Modern Miss Mason* and find their place at the table. Whilst I'll never hide from you who I am or who I follow (you may find the odd Bible story used as an illustration dotted throughout), this book is a spacious place where hopefully you can kick your shoes off, help yourself to a cup of tea, and feel completely at home, whoever you are.

It's like Cooking!

Looking back on those early days of homeschooling discovery, I am reminded of the film *Julie and Julia*, directed by Nora Ephron. The movie tracks the stories of two women from different time periods told via flashbacks and defining moments. The 1950s narrative is about the life of the world-famous chef and cookbook writer Julia Child, played by the inimitable Meryl Streep. By contrast, the 2002 story line follows modern New York blogger Julie Powell, perfectly portrayed by Amy Adams, as she attempts to recreate Julia's delicious recipes in a contemporary context.

As Julie seeks to conquer every meal in *Mastering the Art of French Cooking*[3] from her tiny kitchen in just one year, she begins to form a sense of kinship with Julia Child even though they have never met. It doesn't matter that the modern recipes aren't perfect replicas of the past successes; what matters is the discovery of a generational and universal love of the process of cooking. It has been just like that for me as I have walked with Charlotte over the years. I have been inspired to learn with my children from the wisdom of the woman who pioneered before me.

Not that I have yet recreated in real life the words she laid down on the page, but I have tried to fill my home with the atmosphere and flavours of Charlotte's intentions.

Finding Your Freedom

Whilst writing about the value of Charlotte's methods for today, Susan Schaeffer Macaulay says, "Miss Mason's educational philosophy is not about what someone thought as a Victorian; it is not tied into the past, as if trying to hark back to a golden age. . . . These ideas, being true ones, have an unchangeable underlying pattern (form) and yet give freedom for individual life and practice."[4]

It is through these *unchanging underlying patterns and practices* that my family has navigated our own path and found true freedom. And freedom is the crucial word for me in what I want you to discover here. Whether you have come to this book as a Charlotte Mason newbie or as a homeschool veteran ready for a refreshing, I want to remind you that you are the expert on your own family. You know what's best for your context and culture. You may even be here and have no intention to educate your children at home at all, and I have no doubt you will find plenty of inspiration from these pages for how to build deeper learning connections with your children. I have always believed that the parent is the primary educator of their child, and they get to choose which parts of this responsibility they delegate to others for a season.

This book is your invitation into an adventure; a call to turn a corner on your already incredible journey of parenting and to see the fresh face of an age-old perspective on motherhood, childhood, and education. I believe you have a passion for mothering and are trying so hard to give your children a beautiful childhood. Whether your children are being taught by you or others, I trust that you are joyfully creating a home atmosphere that cultivates curiosity and wonder.

Let me take your hand and show you what I've seen and experienced firsthand through the work of Charlotte Mason. I'll suggest ways you and your children can explore learning through experiences, teach you vocabulary to describe your own learning journey, and help you practically incorporate Charlotte's life-giving philosophy into your home every day.

Charlotte may be a friend of yours already, or this may be your first meeting. May you find meaning in her work and words expressed through my story.

This book is not your how-to guide, but it will be both philosophical and practical. If you look across the internet, there are already huge amounts of readily available instruction on how to use Charlotte's methods; from prepared dictation to picture study. The challenge with this approach is that if we don't start with the big picture and understand the *why* behind the *what*, then we may become proficient at tasks but end up missing the point with our children.

This book is more of a *how to be* than a *how to do*, although I do help ground ideas through a series of "Mason Moments." I'm confident that you are all intelligent, innovative educators who are able to lovingly outwork what you need to in your individual context.

This book isn't a memoir, although I do share personal memories. It doesn't cover every idea, concept, and method, as I don't want to merely replicate the writings of Charlotte that are freely available to read. It's not an academic manifesto, and it most definitely isn't a curriculum. I'm not trying to prove that I'm an expert or that you should do it my way. In fact, I want to say quite the opposite; this book is a signed permission slip to do it your way. This is not a detailed map, but a travel journal to help you choose your own adventure.

Despite my obvious passion for her approach to life, this book isn't intended to be a shrine to Charlotte. Like you, I am free to exclude, include, agree, or disagree with any element of Charlotte's writing and ideas. This doesn't dishonour her work or disrespect her personage; this honours *my* children and the family culture we're creating. She was a human being, albeit a brilliant one, but only human. I am wary of those who interpret her words into shouts of *must* and *should*. If the advice of ancient or modern experts becomes a shackle in our homes, it loses its purpose and intent. We are creative, progressive parents who can weave innovative twenty-first-century ideas and outwork our own application of Charlotte's methods.

We are all Modern Miss Masons. This is about your story, not mine.

Thankfully, you don't need a master's degree in education to start implementing this approach: Charlotte wanted every mother to understand what is possible for them no matter their starting point. You don't have to live somewhere amazing like the Lake District in the UK to put these ideas into practice (but if you do, I am very jealous and would like an invite). You don't have to wait for your ideal set-up or circumstances; you just need to have your own vision. Let's not overthink our life with our children; we have the privilege to walk alongside them as they look, learn, and grow. Let's not compare or complain when our bookshelves aren't colour coded, our printables aren't always bound, or we don't have a rotating display showing off this season's nature finds.

Our family began home educating with very little money (I had to sell books to buy books) and very little space, but we had a huge amount of passion and creativity to use what we had to plant the seeds of a life-giving education. From the moment a child is placed in your arms, whether through birth or adoption, you begin the important role of facilitating their education experience. If ever I ask someone the question "How long have you been home educating?" and the parents answer, "From the beginning," then I know I've found a kindred spirit!

Reframing Childhood, Education, and Motherhood

Charlotte's faithful tenacity to serve children has not just influenced my own homeschooling practice, but it has reframed my understanding of childhood, education, and motherhood. Throughout this book we will unpack these three areas and reframe our understanding through the lens of the Charlotte Mason philosophy.

Childhood

Charlotte has helped me reframe my perspective on childhood by recognising that each child is unique, and thus we can plan their learning journey accordingly. As parents we can create atmospheres, rhythms, and environments that help inspire our children's lives. When we capture the attention of our children, it will help capture the attention of their hearts. And if we can just have the faith to stand back and let children feast on the table of learning we lay before them, it can change their childhood forever.

Education

Through the application of Charlotte's approach to education I have come to understand that we can use tools like narration to encourage personal relevancy and to deepen the child's connection with any subject. We can find treasure in living books that stays with us for a lifetime. We can go outside to explore nature and allow it to be our teacher. As we expose our children to the best of music, art, theatre, and literature, we not only help create lifelong learners but enrich their lives for the better.

Motherhood

Charlotte has inspired me to reframe my perspective on motherhood by recognising that when mothers go out to play and refresh their own bodies and souls, it leads to happier households. We need to see that when we invest in our own minds and stay intellectually alive, we are investing in our children. As mothers discover the power of community, we don't just overcome individual isolation but keep moving the whole Mason movement forward together. By laying a consistent, firm foundation today, we are preparing to impact the next generation tomorrow.

It is these wonderful ideas about childhood, education, and motherhood that we will explore in depth in the three sections of this book.

More Than Just the Ingredients

During this writing process I have conducted countless hours of research beyond my repeated reading of Charlotte Mason's volumes to add flavour and variety to your experience. Some of this work has influenced large elements of the chapters you'll read, some just made it into a sentence. I have found that reading widely around Charlotte Mason's work (practitioners' perspectives, academic papers, modern books on education/habits, etc.) only deepens my understanding of her ideas and has enabled me to put the philosophy into practice uniquely and creatively. My hope is that reading this book does that for you.

Quite ironically, I encountered one of the most poignant articles I read in this process whilst at the hairdressers. I was reading my favourite magazine called *The Simple Things*. The article I found myself reading was about the secret of Syrian cooking:

> There are two indispensable ingredients in Syrian cooking. Sumac, the deep-red spice brought to Syria on the Silk Road, and nafas, which literally means "breath"—but in relation to food means "the art of cooking where ingredients combine harmoniously." Nafas is knowing how to get the best from the season's harvest or how to use a perfectly ripe tomato. Nafas is the highest compliment you can give a Syrian cook. Nafas

is found in the heart of the person at the stove and in the essence of a well-prepared dish.[5]

Upon exploring this concept further, I discovered a *New York Times* article about how the heart and soul of Syrian cooking is derived from childhood memories; the *nafas* here is described as "energy" and "intimacy," and is all about what the individual imparts to the food.

A concept used mostly to describe home cooks, not chefs, nafas speaks to a certain intimacy that stretches beyond the physical attributes of a dish. It is about the person preparing it, and what she imparts to the food. It is the time and energy spent selecting and preparing the ingredients; the patient dance back and forth with seasonings until every flavor is just right; the generous presentation and warm hospitality; and, above all, the love of cooking and the desire to feed others.[6]

This beautiful word, *nafas*, has helped me understand my ongoing journey with Charlotte Mason as a growth agent for how I view motherhood, childhood, and education. My aim has always been to learn all I can, then bring the elements together harmoniously.

I have come to realise that homeschooling, like Syrian cooking, is more than just the sum of its ingredients. We can have all the Charlotte Mason books on our shelves, and we might even read them. We can share the same pretty planning pages, curriculum choices, or joy in using old educational methods, but as the saying goes, "the proof is in the pudding." The heart and soul of moving freely comes from slowly sitting with the tools and ideas, growing alongside our children, and observing their whimsical ways. We learn to freely accept what comes naturally and reject what doesn't fit with our unique family expression and values. Educational nafas is found in the heart of the person in the homeschool room and in the essence of a well-prepared educational feast.

When I talk about finding your freedom, I might be misunderstood as implying you should have no structure or intention, or even be misconstrued as being against using set plans or curriculums. Those who know me and have followed along with my journey over the past two decades of being a parent know that this isn't necessarily the case! I'm all about the "whole person" experience for the parent and child. I'm an advocate for you not being baffled or bound by the *shoulds* of the educational world; rather I would encourage you to be well read, informed, inspired, and led by the family and context you experience every day. Therefore, I want you to embrace *how to be* before you commence with your *what to do*. I am not against using other people's recipes, but I am for you finding your nafas.

The future of Charlotte Mason's ideas won't be found in a prepackaged curriculum, someone else's ideas, or printed sheets that can be ticked off. These elements may help set us on our way, but finding our freedom and firming up the future for ourselves and the next generation lies with the "home cooks," not the experts and academics. It's about your heart, soul, and physical preparations and what you impart to your child's learning days. It's the time and energy you spend selecting and preparing the environment, the books, and the experiences. It's that patient dance back and forth, from one child to another, from one subject to the next, until every aspect is placed with peace and offered with warm hospitality. The secret ingredient is found in the love of the family and your desire to lay out the opportunity for a unique but incredible, full life for your children.

My greatest hope is that no matter how you find your way, what you use to guide your days, or what you hang your rhythms upon, you too can find your nafas with the help of this book.

Through these pages, may you truly find the confidence to continue.

Part 1

Reframing Childhood

Chapter 1

Raising Humans

Children are born persons.

CHARLOTTE MASON, *A PHILOSOPHY OF EDUCATION*

Charlotte Mason's first transforming principle argues that children are born persons. Each child is born unique with character, innate personality, gifts, and raw abilities. As parents and educators, we must learn to be curious about who they are in order to help them become who they are destined to be.

Changing Our View of Children

Every baby has an origin story. The day my parents brought me home from the hospital for the first time, lightning struck our next-door neighbor's chimney. It was a hot August afternoon in 1975, and I had clearly made an electric first impression on the world! I am lovingly told that I was born with a tooth, a gorgeous mop of hair, and was considered "a good weight." This was the beginning of my story, and my parents have retold their first impressions of me affectionately time and time again.

Each of my four children has their unique tale of arrival, which they still secretly love to hear about. There are story beats we reutter around birthdays and milestones to mark their starting point. For my first-born daughter, it was me blurting out spontaneously, "I knew it was you!" through exhausted tears as I held her for the first time. For our youngest son, it was the midwife's loud exclamation upon his sudden entrance into our living room, declaring with excitement, "Wow, he has so much hair!" My husband even proudly recounts that he cut the umbilical cord of each of our children, as if it allows him to take credit for the births themselves. He somehow edits out the fact that straight after our third child was born, he went down with a fever and was laid in bed for three days straight.

Understanding our origin story is important for shaping our sense of identity, purpose, and belonging. Whether our story starts with tears of pain or joy, most of our personal history is passed down to us like an oral tradition or a family recipe. In a culture where parents live-stream moment-by-moment accounts of their child's birth across social media, it is comforting to be reminded what an intimate experience it can be to hold our offspring in our arms and tell them the tale of their birth.

Our journey into this world starts with us blindly unaware of ourselves. As our life story unfolds by oral recollection, the voices we listen to begin to draw out who we are and influence how we will play our part in the world. By contrast, when parents neglect the practice of recollection and storytelling, children may experience great pain whilst wrestling with a lack of identity, since it has not been shaped by a trusted parental figure. These initial years of a child's life are critical in laying the foundation for the years to follow.

Charlotte believed the uniqueness of every one of our babies must be the foundation of reframing childhood, education, and motherhood. The first important principle that shaped her educational theory was the phrase: "Children are born *persons*."[1] Out of the twenty principles that her philosophy hinged on, none was considered more vital than this one.

The essence of the *born person* concept is that when a child comes into the world, they are not a project without a blueprint, a raw piece of wood to be whittled, or a lump of clay to be moulded. They are instead born as a *whole person*: full of life, personality, and the capacity and capability to engage with the world. In simple terms, every child comes with preloaded software that cannot be ignored or easily overridden. Each unique character is born with innate personality, a set of talents, gifts, and raw abilities. We must work with what the child has, not against it; or, in Charlotte's words, we "are limited by the respect due to the personality of children, which must not be encroached upon, whether by the direct use of fear or love, suggestion or influence, or by undue play upon any one natural desire."[2]

The born person approach sees children as complete human beings from the moment we hear their first cry. Rather than dictate who they should be, we learn to participate in who they already are. In this, we give children value and a voice. We honour them as human beings from day one, which has a transformational impact on both their present and future selves. This idea is crucial, as it shapes Charlotte's entire educational approach. Without viewing children as born persons, we cannot fully engage in her teachings.

I have had the privilege of guiding many mothers into home education over the years, and for any who desire to integrate the Charlotte Mason approach, I always start with the born persons idea.

Believing our children are born whole and as a complete person doesn't mean we suddenly let go, throwing our arms up in the air and exclaiming, "Whatever will be will be." As we hold that 8 lb., 3 oz. bundle of gorgeousness in our arms for the very first time, we're not just holding a person, but also the responsibility for their possibility. We can't control or manipulate their lives, but we can lay down tracks of love, apply rich stimuli, and foster an environment for them to think and speak up, grow, and explore. Mothers are privileged to get a front-row seat at our born person's great unveiling.

Transforming Our Perspective on Education

Whilst there have been many modern advances in science, technology, and psychology since Charlotte Mason's day, current evidence continues to reinforce her notion that every child has an innate ability to think, to communicate, and to be curious as a fully formed human. However, it seems that society still needs reminders of this at times.

Parents may believe in principle that their child is uniquely formed, yet in practice they can succumb to society's pressure to dictate what their child needs to know and who their child needs to be. We default to teaching our children disconnected facts rather than helping them build a personalised knowledge base tailored to their own specific personality and future pathway.

Two children can emerge from the same public school with widely disparate results—demonstrating that the same input can lead to totally different outputs. Mass education has led to shortcuts and assumptions and a standardisation that doesn't work for every child, because the way every child learns is different. Rather than ignore differences and seek to homogenise childhood, we as parents and educators can instead become curious to understand the wonder of our child's diversity. In short, we study the child to help the child study. Many parents realise too late that their child does not fit the box they've spent years constructing for them. We can avoid this by attentively curating the atmosphere of a child's life to help draw out who he or she already is.

Back in the nineteenth century, children were supposed to be seen and not heard. The first modern education system had an inherent babysitting mentality, intimating that students' real value began when they entered the factory workforce or the local coal pit. Classrooms were set up with the view that all children began at the same starting point. Educators aimed for a standardised outcome of information retention, not individualised learning.

Some parents today would argue that little has changed since the Victorian era. Some might say we still live in a babysitter society where institutions, digital technology, and even Sunday schools are seeking to do the work for us or, at the least, keep a child occupied, entertained, and busy until the child becomes useful. Yet having such low expectations of children leads to simplifying their learning environment. We can unintentionally keep children at a stereotypical age rather than an individual learning stage.

Our methodology is always a reflection of our ideology. We must ask ourselves, What do we really believe about the nature of children?

Whilst much of the Victorian era's education prepared young people for the workforce, school looked different for children of wealthy families. A governess would offer the upper-class children lessons in music and art and languages that, in turn, benefitted the child's education and understanding of the world. Meanwhile, the children in the lower classes received only the minimal basics of reading, writing, and arithmetic.

An important premise of the born person approach is that people of every background and status should have access to a wide curriculum and the freedom to search for knowledge. Each child is worthy of "a liberal education for all,"[3] which includes a spacious environment to learn in, books and toys to explore for themselves, and adults around them ready to listen and engage with their learning journey.

In the last two decades of her life, Charlotte published volumes on education and poetry and wrote inspirational living books for children. She pioneered a national education union and started a training college for teachers and governesses in Ambleside, and her work was being recognised all around the world. Charlotte desired to bring a transformational shift to the nature of education itself. She was on a mission to close the gap between the rich and poor, creating a system that worked for the whole of society, not just the handpicked elite. She wanted all children to be exposed to great art, inspiring music, and the best thinkers of the time. Every child should be offered the opportunity to feed their curiosity in whatever direction their natural inclinations might take them. Charlotte's questioning of the status quo was founded on her revolutionary thinking about children and their place in the world.

Charlotte knew if the educators, parents, and influencers changed what they thought about children, it could ultimately liberate generations to come. No matter if children came from wealth or poverty, they would know they were whole and they had a voice in the world. They would see they were free to learn from the same thinkers, writers, and creators as anyone else.

Adopting a born person approach deeply challenges our thinking and motives about education itself.

If you're visiting our home and need to use the bathroom facilities downstairs, you are required to walk through our home library/home-schooling space. One weekend a friend came to visit and noticed a few books still out and open from Friday's reading; she spotted *Beautiful Stories from Shakespeare* by Edith Nesbit on the desk and exclaimed, "You read Shakespeare to your children already?" I quickly responded with a "Yes, why wouldn't I?" and began enthusiastically sharing the delights of the Shakespearean language and lessons from his stories. I would have gone on for longer until her body reminded her why she was walking through the library in the first place! Our conversation challenged my friend's ideas about her children being "too young" for seemingly advanced literature or ideas, yet a born person approach lays down limitations and opens up children to a more generous world of learning.

Within a few weeks my friend had bought a set of Shakespeare stories for her children, who were devouring them at bedtime.

Developing Childlike Curiosity about Children

As a young mother, I felt quite overwhelmed at the thought of raising and educating four different individuals.

In the first few weeks of homeschooling I discovered a Charlotte Mason–style programme that "everyone" seemed to be using. I scoured the website, created an Excel spreadsheet with each child's name at the top of a column, and attempted to design a bespoke, individual timetable of study for each child. If I told you I got to week two, I'd be stretching the truth; I think by day three I opened my spreadsheet (already behind) and felt immediately overwhelmed at my own expectations. I closed my computer, told the children to grab their wellies and coats, and we headed to the park to explore the park instead. On returning we made hot chocolate and snuggled up around E. B. White's *Charlotte's Web*, followed by oral retellings, creative play, and the children enthusiastically asking, "Mum, when are we going to read the next chapter?"

What I learnt over time is that I could offer the same stimuli, read the same books, and ask the same questions of each of my children, but I couldn't expect the same outcome. Each of my children interacted with themes, poets, composers, artists, and great thinkers with individuality. One would see the detailed background in a painting, whilst another would find hidden meaning in the wider picture. One would delight in dates, descriptions, and the details of a story, and another would focus on the behaviour of a character. As we give the same inputs, we learn much about who each child is by observing and hypothesizing why they express such different outputs.

Charlotte referred to the early developing years (we may know them as preschool) as a "quiet growing time."[4] This period of a child's life is full of accelerated learning and development. We see a child progress from a milk-hungry babe in arms to a walking, talking (opinionated) small human ready to take on the world. Charlotte encouraged us to stand back and allow these developmental stages to take place without ineffective parental prodding, pushing, or provoking. We learn to trust our children to learn on their own.

I was recently speaking to a first-time mother who was processing with me the wonder of watching a little human discover everything for the first time. "I'm just fascinated by her!" she exclaimed. "I could watch her forever." The wonders of childhood and motherhood are so intrinsically intertwined. Just as a newborn child is curiously discovering their new environment, so we must develop curiosity about our children. It is from this place of wonder and attention that we can actively create an environment where they can fully become who they were born to be. As our mindset around children adjusts, our actions will inevitably follow.

No matter how long I have been a parent, I'm still fascinated by not only my children's personalities and how they work (or don't quite work) alongside mine, but I'm also fascinated by how my friends' growing children develop before our eyes. A born person attitude changes how we celebrate children themselves, whether they are ours or not. I have a friend called Ann who is loved and adored by children. Whenever I am around her, I am always struck by how she talks about and to children. She refers to them as "little people," looking them in the eye and giving them both value and a voice. This phrase "little people" acknowledges their need for protection but still marks their individual presence and personhood. No wonder the children love her so much—they always feel seen and heard around her.

The born person perspective has shaped all of my interactions with children; I now try to make it my mission to be interested in other people's children, not just my own. Consider how often we default to speaking babbling nonsense to a child or reducing them to decoration by saying, "Isn't she cute," and then move on with adult concerns and conversation. The children often sit around us rather than *with* us. We can build a positive parenting culture by talking to children directly and taking time to enter their world. Remember our opening story with Pam and the sloppy joes? The nature of the children I met that day in the cafeteria may indicate that the significant adults in their lives were acting on this advice.

When we ask a child how they are doing, we can build deeper connections with the child quickly. And when we ask fellow parents what they are enjoying about their children and what they notice about them, we motivate those parents to feel more curiosity themselves about their young ones.

We were recently spending time with another family, and after eating dinner in the garden, most of the younger children were engaged with outdoor games. Their youngest daughter, however, was more interested in hanging out with the adults. This three-year-old explorer began collecting unripe damson fruits that had fallen from a tree and bringing them to me. Any attempts at adult conversation were soon overtaken by child's play. We sat and arranged the growing number of fruits on the table. Each time, she would slowly count them out and proudly announce the number to me with a grin on her face. This went on until we had over ten damson fruits laid out before us. The game only finished after we hid the fruit in different-shaped garden pots. This wonderful little girl was then happy enough to go and join her siblings. Nature had just given us a free lesson in mathematics. Meanwhile, I had a lesson from a young girl who was growing into an inquisitive, confident little person who would no doubt make use of whatever she could get her hands on in the future.

Attentively observing young personalities can help us foresee what kind of persons they might become as teens and adults. Charlotte suggests that spotting our children's distinct character traits early helps us observe how their behaviours could have "possibilities for good and for evil."[5] A tenacious stubbornness in a young child could either wreak havoc in future relationships, or it could be a catalyst for change in the world through social justice. Artist and dancer Stacia Tauscher is known for saying that, when considering our children's potential, "we worry about what a child will be tomorrow, yet we forget that he is someone today."[6] Our role is to help children navigate childhood today, whilst learning to discern who they are to help bring out the best in them in the future.

Such curiosity will lead to acknowledging our children's perspective on the world. My children are completely different from me; I love their growing personalities and characters, but I often find their differences stark. My children don't think like me and don't always see the world like I do, but that doesn't stop me from showing it to them. They are growing up in a world seemingly more complex than I ever experienced, but they are resilient and observant, and I am learning to pay attention to *their* world, so I get to walk alongside them in it.

Trusting That Seeds Will Bear Fruit

I've always wanted to live in a house that had fruit trees in the garden. My mother wisely mentored me not to wait until you buy the perfect house in the future, but rather just plant something right where you are. So, a couple of years ago, I planted cherry, plum, apple, and pear trees around our home. The trees are correctly labelled, and I've faithfully tended and watered them at the right time. And now I wait patiently for the blossoms to appear each spring. To be honest, thus far my only yield has been a couple of perfect-looking pears growing in readiness for an autumn harvest. But I haven't lost heart. The trees are growing, they are firmly planted and rooted, and I trust fruit will come. I guess in both planting and parenting, trust plays a huge part in allowing fruit to come forth.

Take sunflower seeds, for instance. Every packet is labelled with detailed planting instructions. If we follow them correctly, we'll enjoy the fruit of our labour, but we can't change or control the outcome of the seed we planted. If you plant a sunflower seed, you'll eventually get a sunflower growing in your garden. If you plant an apple tree, you'll eventually get apples. There is no guessing game here; you get what you plant! We simply need to water what is already there. This is key to the born person approach to parenting and education. As Susan Schaeffer Macaulay puts it, "Do not see him as something to prune, form, or mold. This is an individual who thinks, acts, and feels. He is a separate human being whose strength lies in who he is, not in who he will become."[7]

During the summer months, I try to get into the daily routine of an early morning walk in the park that sits at our doorstep and is accessible by our very own secret garden gate. As the late June sun takes its place in the sky, the local wildflowers always catch my attention much more than linear, perfectly planted flower gardens. There's something endearing about the dispersal of scattered seed—the surprise of their varied shapes and colours and the freedom of their movement in the wind. The flowers stand strong and beautiful, feeding and nourishing both the bees and my soul every morning.

We can learn a valuable lesson about raising children from the wildflowers in our park. Many times, we obsess over how our children will turn out, as if our internal worry can somehow reorder their external behaviour. We try to overcontrol the "soil" of their environment to keep them from being choked by life's weeds. We endlessly try to prune and shape their growth to look according to our plan or the blueprint of culture. Yet the real planting of our children simply requires an atmosphere of scattered love, some wildly colourful nurturing, and the ability to trust their roots will let them grow.

Cultivating Their Divine Spark

Christians believe that children (as all humans) are created *imago Dei*, in the image of God—a divine spark from the source of light. It's fair to say that the parents' mindset, convictions, and belief system will have a huge influence on how they apply Charlotte's principle that children are born persons. As Charlotte was a woman of faith, it would be remiss of me to describe her first principle without touching on her encouragement for us to never separate the life of a child from their Creator. She believed that from the moment of their divinely appointed entrance into this life, every child has instant access to God's world, to observe and interact with it in wide-eyed wonder.

Our convictions, faith based or otherwise, don't change the core of who the child is, but they do impact the atmospheres we create, the daily rhythms we lead our children in, and the feast of education we lay out. In this sense, it is important to know what we believe, as our personal mindset can help or hinder a child's growth.

Children often emulate what they see those around them doing. They pick up on our perspective. If we're sleepily going through the days, keeping children entertained or busy and counting down to bed-time, then our children will feel like an inconvenience. But if we're joyfully reading with them, engaging in their world, and relishing their company, they will see life is for them to live and interact with too.

Believing our children are "born persons" is liberating and comfort-ing even when it becomes stretching and uncomfortable. It encourages a sense of awe and wonder as we stand back and watch their God-given potential unfold. Belief in who they are is the essence of this approach to raising humans. I can't control, I can't compare, and I must see them in the context of who they are, not through my idealised (or rose-tinted) glasses. Through this lens, I am learning to let go but love deeper; love with hindsight and foresight; love with their life in mind and not mine; love with hope, not idealism. I'm raising a person, not a prototype that I can adjust and tweak along the way if it doesn't go to plan.

Childhood is not a waiting game. These young minds and lives are not merely passing time until they are "useful" to the world, as believed formerly by some Victorian educators. They are to be very present, whole, valued, and celebrated right now.

We shouldn't hold our hands up and surrender all responsibility to fate. We don't throw caution to the wind and mutter, "Whatever will be will be." We let go of pressurized dictation and embrace active participation. We seek to be sources of inspiration who walk alongside children and help them find the treasure of knowledge that was meant for them with solutions they can tie into the story of their lives. As we observe the divine spark in them, we begin to understand who they really are and the valuable part they play in the world. We learn to celebrate raising humans who will add to the grand story of all our lives.

TAKE A MASON MOMENT:
Suggestions for Embedding a Born Person Approach

- Become an observer of your children; it seems obvious, but getting to know their personality traits from a young age is fascinating and fun! Take some time to write down what you see in each of your children, what you enjoy about them, and what you see developing in them.
- Speak to children about their individuality: encourage them with words such as "I love how curious/observant/creative you are!"

- Listen to a child's questions. Write them down if you can't answer them straight away; it's a helpful insight into what's going on in their mind.
- Consider your children before you consider your curriculum.
- Listen and pay attention when your children are narrating their day; as much as it's tempting to fold laundry whilst they tell historic tales, it doesn't convey how important their retellings are.
- Remember, one rule doesn't fit all. Consider this when making decisions about varying aspects of your children's lives.
- Share each child's "story" (birth or beginnings) with them; it develops a wonderful sense of individuality and uniqueness within a family.
- Allocate time in your schedule for each child to practise something that expresses their individuality; for example, learning Adobe Photoshop, attending a drama club, or riding a mountain bike off-road.
- As your children get into their teen years and express ideas around future careers or pathways, begin to orientate parts of their learning focus to specialize in subjects relevant for their journey.
- Read through Charlotte Mason's original six volumes over an extended period to gain a deeper understanding of how seeing your children as born persons can truly transform your home.

Chapter 2

Laying Foundations

We are limited to three educational instruments—
the atmosphere of environment,
the discipline of habit,
and the presentation of living ideas.

CHARLOTTE MASON, *A PHILOSOPHY OF EDUCATION*

Charlotte Mason shaped her practices around a simple motto for parents that made a difference for children: atmosphere, discipline, and life. These are the tools of the trade, the three golden elements we can gently cultivate. These educational foundations are not dependent on wealth, experience, or academic accolades; rather they are accessible to every family and every child, and they can be outworked in the light of any child's growth and development.

A Motto That Matters

The so-called parents' motto, presented by Charlotte Mason, describes education as an "atmosphere, a discipline, and a life."[1] These three essential components do not exist in isolation but rather work together as part of a holistic educational approach. The motto seeks to set up a paradigm that we can then adapt to our own family culture. Here we get the opportunity to consider the ideas and values that already rule our lives and homes (the atmosphere), the habits and rhythms that shape our day and our character (the discipline), and the books we use to provide living stimuli to bring out the best and unique qualities in our children (the life). Although our natural focus may lean towards the child, we first need to consider ourselves as adults in the picture. In so many ways this approach is about who we are as humans before it is about who we are as educators.

Becoming a Parent Who Cultivates the Atmosphere

I wasn't home educated, but I still learnt my greatest lessons from home.

A normal day would start with me waking up to the sound of music playing softly from the dining room or kitchen, where my parents were starting their day; I'd come downstairs to find my mum reading her Bible and maybe a candle lit on the mantelpiece. I'd rush to use the shower before school—and before my siblings—where I'd be greeted by a Renoir print on the back of the bathroom door. More often than not I knew we wouldn't be alone around the dinner table—my mum always stretched dinner out and invited others in.

My very normal home and upbringing instilled a love for God, for hospitality, for music, for books, for art, for singing, for nature, and much more. These things weren't in a curriculum or planned strategically throughout the week; we didn't sign up for a subscription box, or ever have the money for private classes—they were simply our life. Or to be more precise, they were my parents' life first. Atmosphere was just there, hanging in the air, ready for me to pluck, play with, and place in my life forever.

Charlotte taught that atmosphere comes from the ideas that rule our lives: children breathe in these ideas and then pattern their lives upon them. The atmosphere of our home grows from our beliefs about faith and the future, our shared political views, the news we read, the books we savour, and the parts of life we value and hold dear. Charlotte describes the atmosphere as being "about the child, his natural element, precisely as the atmosphere of the earth is about us."[2] Charlotte further says that "it is thrown off, as it were, from persons and things, stirred by events, sweetened by love, ventilated, kept in motion, by the regulated action of common sense."[3]

Charlotte believed that the type of atmosphere we create is key to a child's education, whether in the classroom or at home, and that the parent or educator must do their utmost to curate and cultivate their own lives to help children under their care thrive and learn.

When I was younger, I was always aware of the different smells my friends' homes had, not necessarily bad or good but just different. When we moved into our first home in Coventry with our young children, there was one cupboard, the one under the stairs, which no matter what we did still smelt of the wonderful old lady who had lived there before us!

Consider how different nations have unique cultures, formed from their special traditions, symbols, ceremonies, values, belief systems, and relational connections that we don't even notice are there until a friend from another country points them out to us. In a way our homes are like little countries, each having their own strands of cultural DNA that are intangibly transmitted to our children.

The concept of atmosphere is often confused with the more familiar idea of creating an educational "environment" for our children. With no end of Pinterest inspiration on how to set up a space for your family with walls lined and layered with phonics posters and times tables charts, it's no wonder we feel the pressure to get it perfect. I have read many online forum questions from new homeschooling mothers asking about how to set up the classroom in their home. Whilst it can be a useful practical question, it should never be a primary one. Fashioning a beautiful homeschool set-up is not the same as creating an atmosphere.

If the culture of the home is created by what is intentionally formed and seen, then the tone of the home is what is heard and transferred. The atmosphere of your home is formed intentionally by how you lead as parents. It is shaped by clear, consistent communication in the intimate safe spaces where repetition and rhythm make all the difference. How we speak and what we speak about matters. What isn't said in a home is often as important as what is; silence speaks volumes. We can cultivate consistency by demonstrating what matters through our actions, by celebrating that which we know to be good, whilst challenging that which is not. Culture is so contagious that we inevitably catch it from each other. We just need to make sure we are the ones setting the tone.

Whilst children often interact with many other adults (whether from classes, church, sports, or youth groups), research shows that parents still have the most influence in a child's life. In one of my previous professions (before I was a mother) I worked with children in our local school system who had challenges with emotional or behavioural issues. These issues often made it difficult for them to gain the most benefit from their learning environment (the classroom). I supported these children through one-on-one mentoring and group meetings. Many of these disadvantaged children were on the verge of being excluded from the school system, so I was sent in for a final intervention before they were deemed unsuitable for school. I was the one who sought to give them an opportunity to process the reasons they were constantly being thrown out of the classroom!

I remember working with one boy (we'll call him Ray) who came to school so dirty I had to bring wipes with me to every session so he could wash his hands and arms before we started. I'd start most morning sessions with "It's nice to see you, Ray, have you eaten today?" His uniform was covered in dog hair and went unwashed or changed for weeks, and during a session where he was telling me about an incident that had happened at home, I discovered that he didn't have a bed and he slept with his dogs. I learnt that Ray's dogs were very important to him and provided comfort; this knowledge framed many of our conversations and developments over my months of work with him.

Session after session my heart broke for these children. Many had even basic needs that weren't being met (whether food, suitable shelter, or a loving and present parent); therefore listening to a mathematics teacher or answering a science question in a loud classroom with thirty other children was the least of their priorities. My work was fulfilling but also hugely disappointing as I grew to realise that I could never be greater than the influence of their home life. I had to trust that the tone of encouragement and openness I created for just a few hours a week, the kind words spoken over these children, and the time given to them had sown seeds in their lives somehow—and just hope for their safety and care in the long run. I was reminded in that tough role that the potency of our home life is more powerful than any educational programme or tool.

A few years ago, my children and I were learning about the different types of lichen found around the parks and woodland area where we live, and one feature of lichen helped me understand Charlotte's notion of atmosphere. Lichen is very sensitive to the atmosphere around it; it is a good determiner for clean (or polluted) air. If the air is very badly polluted with sulphur dioxide, then lichen may not be present at all, or just green algae may be found. But if the air is clean, then shrubby, hairy, and leafy lichens become abundant. The impact of the atmosphere of our homes may not be abundantly clear from day to day, but growth and development happen over a lifetime. If we keep doing the good work and setting an example of integrity, beauty, and grace, then maybe our children will become shrubby, hairy, leafy, and abundant!

Mother's Day, or Mothering Sunday as we call it here in the UK, falls in March; just as the light is returning and the morning frost is lessening. I love that my children are now getting older and using their own money to buy gifts without a prompting from their father! This means I now receive slightly more upmarket gifts than glitter-drowned rainbows and cutout paper hearts (although I did love those too!). Even more meaningful to me than the gifts are the cards my children give me, now full of words which are more than just a beautiful inscription of their first name. On one occasion my daughters found me crying over my croissant with a card in one hand and an annotated video montage on my phone, from my youngest, in the other. Both daughters focused on how I have taught them to see beauty, to notice nature, and to choose thankfulness over everything. One daughter wrote, "We thank you for teaching us in the most beautiful way possible how to live life in radical amazement, to live life for Jesus, and how to capture the beauty of life whether that is in words, photos, or actions."

Through many years of intentionally creating the atmosphere of our home, I never imagined my first formal review coming in the way of a Mother's Day card—mothers rarely get feedback on our role. Our rewards usually come as we see our children creating their own atmospheres, which they've intangibly caught from ours. Atmosphere is like low-hanging fruit and our children are the harvesters, gathering piece by piece for a bountiful yield.

Becoming a Parent Who Creates Rhythm

I'm a huge proponent of establishing healthy building blocks for life through a nurtured home and childhood. Charlotte was right about many things, but she was also writing over a century ago. Today, our understandings of science, physiology, and child development have progressed somewhat, and I believe Charlotte would be the first to say "Lean in and listen" to new discoveries, fresh research, and current writers in this area. There are online lists, suggestions, and tips available aplenty on "habit training" our children, but the responsibility and choice lie with you. Our children have varying abilities, our families have different expectations, and we will all have contrasting outcomes.

We've now had over a century of scientific research and writing from neuroscience, psychology, and beyond discussing this area of habits since Charlotte first formed her own thoughts. For example, in his helpful and practical book *Tiny Habits*, writer BJ Fogg lays out the idea that to create a new habit requires three simple things: the motivation to do it, the ability to master it, and a prompt to remember it.[4] Because our motivation often only lasts if the positive feelings of starting something new also last, we have to perform small actions consistently if we want to see long-term change happen. Little changes make a big difference when it comes to forming habits that last.

We decided as a family to home educate because we wanted to be able to explore a world of learning that wasn't skewed by an overfocus on grading or testing. We wanted to give our children the permission to learn at their own stage and age. At first, I thought enforcing regular habits might grate against the freedom I desired my children to have, but I now think that the concept of establishing repeated rhythms and healthy structures does make sense if we want to succeed in helping our children become attentive, observant learners. Charlotte believed that helping children embed habits in their life would not only help the culture of the home but also develop the heart and character of a child for many years to come. She believed in the proverb "to train up a child in the way they should go,"[5] and this inevitably means tackling the challenge to encourage habits that last. The language of rhythm and repetition may sit gentler with you and your children rather than habit and discipline. Remember language creates culture, so use what sits right with you.

Habits of the hand are the practical domestic rhythms we teach our children, such as emptying the dishwasher or picking up toys, or even helping them remember to brush their teeth. Parents often feel a great deal of pressure for our homes to be perfect, whilst simultaneously struggling to be consistent with the habits we are trying to instill in our children! Whilst it's not really a big deal if every room of the house is not always Instagram-ready, we can't lead our children in habit formation if we don't set the example for them to follow. That's why I'm all in favour of learning *alongside* our children. My children have seen me struggle with organisation and order but have observed my breakthroughs, too. I'm open about my domestic inabilities, but I also communicate the possibility of change and progress.

After fighting with my inabilities for years and stressfully (and speedily) wiping down the bathroom and kitchen before visitors came over, I decided to get a cleaner. After my decision to follow Jesus and saying yes to Dave Boden when he asked me to marry him, this is definitely one of the best and most life-changing decisions I've ever made! Am I exaggerating? Absolutely not! I remember how on the day when I informed my children of this angelic visitor who was going to be gracing our home for a couple of hours a week, they responded with "Yay, we don't have to do chores anymore," to which I responded, "Aha, no—our cleaner is coming to help Mum because I'm focusing on homeschooling, operationally running our home, and writing; sometimes to make things better we have to ask for help. We will continue to keep our home tidy; our new friend will help keep it clean."

What I've found is that with the cleaning aspect of our home covered, I can focus on operations and organisation. I suddenly had mind space for meal planning, monthly bulk buying, and cooking from scratch most evenings. A definite win!

The parent's example is of high importance, because whatever we say to our children ultimately comes down to the power of emulation of pattern; they do what they see. So, what do they see in you?

If you are in the habit of doing something, you do it regularly and repeatedly, almost without thinking about it. Yet good habits rarely form automatically and often take intentional work to put into practice. Though I have diligently worked to cultivate practical habits that were helpful to our household in a particular season, I've found it is incredibly easy for a child to give up on them when given the opportunity or excuse! Young children may not have a strong, burning, intrinsic desire to empty the dishwasher for you or even pick up their own socks because they don't always see why they need to do it. Therefore, when it comes to the long-term development of deeper habits, we must find ways to motivate beyond just compliance with our instruction.

When working on establishing habits, it's important to remember that there's no expectation without explanation. A task must be explained and patterned clearly, repeatedly, and with joy, if a child is to find the motivation for it and skill to succeed in it. Creating a prompt or reminder in their routine can help them to remember what needs to be done. As some of my own children are becoming adults, I can finally see in them a fresh motivation to domesticate their world. Old habits are beginning to reemerge; I guess when you can't see your bedroom floor and you have nothing to wear, you finally hear your mother's voice from deep within reminding you about the blessing of order and cleanliness! The question here isn't how teaching children the discipline of habits can help improve your life; it's how can teaching them helpful habits empower theirs?

Habits of the heart are the attitudes, values, and relational connections that we express on a consistent basis. Most parents are now deeply concerned about their children growing up to be kind, loving, and emotionally intelligent—as much as or more than they want them to be clever. We want to raise our children to be empathic, observant, and caring. Charlotte felt that "habits of gentleness, courtesy, kindness, candour, respect for other people, or—habits quite other than these, are inspired by the child as the very atmosphere of his home, the air he lives in and must grow by."[6]

We have a regular rhythm in our home that we call Morning Time. This can go from being beautifully staged to completely scattered across the span of a week. I've learnt to gather resources for Morning Time together in one place, and it always involves food! This naturally started in our early homeschooling days by reading to the children over breakfast and eventually evolved into a "thing" that's just expected to happen as they come downstairs on weekday mornings. It involves gathering around the table for Bible study, prayer, and reading whilst adding to this regular schedule additional rotating activities such as poetry recitation, listening to classical music, or memorisation. This morning rhythm is a place where conversation flows, values are developed, and children's hearts are enriched. It helps us rise above the ebbs and flows of emotion and energy level. These kinds of routines are catalysts of character in the lives of the younger generation. You and I have this incredible opportunity to strengthen the souls of our sons and daughters through the habits of the heart we help them embed for life.

Becoming a Parent Who Provides Living Ideas

If the *atmosphere* is understood as the invisible bonds that guide us, and *discipline* describes the rhythms and repetitions that last, then *life* grows out from the environment of ideas that are taken from tangible living voices, books, and "things" we place around us. The idea that "education is a life" is often misunderstood or interpreted as "everything is educational," which gives room or justification to be fluid, unintentional, and relaxed about our teachable moments and resources. Whilst I do believe that most things can be educational opportunities, the word *life* here suggests that which is alive, organic, and can multiply. It is about what we invest in our homes to bring out the best in our children.

As a conversation starter to get to know new people, I love to ask them to think of five interesting people they would invite to a dinner party. They could be dead or alive, famous, or otherwise. For me I would have C. S. Lewis, Madeleine L'Engle, Mary Oliver, Maya Angelou, and of course Charlotte Mason around my table. Which five would you choose?

I asked my youngest daughter this question, and she answered Olivia Rodrigo, Sky Brown (young British Japanese Olympic skateboard champion), Zac Efron, Corrie ten Boom, and the dancing dog from *Britain's Got Talent*! Now that's a party I definitely want to attend! We may not be able to literally invite people from the past to be guests in our house, but through the power of books, stories, and publications, we can be inspired by them from afar almost as if they were to come and live amongst us.

Charlotte believed that anything (particularly any book) that was to be used as a resource for a child's education must come from the mind of a great thinker straight to the mind of the child. A living education is wide, varied, and generous. Books by passionate authors and firsthand experiences leave room for the child to explore knowledge and take away what really matters to them. Charlotte wanted children to come away with living ideas instead of dry facts, which are so often found in typical textbooks. Just as we naturally invite certain guests into our homes because of how they will influence the atmosphere within it, so too we can open an invitation for history to enter our world through thinkers of the past. Encouraging parents to raise their children's expectation for deeper thinking, Charlotte says this:

> Treat children in this reasonable way, mind to mind; not so
> much the mind of the teacher to that of the child . . . but the
> minds of a score of thinkers who meet the children, mind
> to mind, in their several books, the teacher performing the
> graceful office of presenting the one enthusiastic mind to
> the other.[7]

Charlotte suggests that those facilitating the learning environment can "present" master writers, composers, and creators to our children as fellow thinkers. Our children may not be contemporaries with them in time, space, and experience, but their capacity to imagine, dream, and discover is no different at all. Although Charlotte felt that books were a high priority for communicating thought, she also wanted to introduce children to the great minds of men and women as communicated through art, music, poetry, and plays. At the end of the day, each one of these creative genres is an invitation to meet real people and find real connections with our world. We open the doors of great thought and discovery for the future by thoughtfully examining the ideas that have shaped the past.

Charlotte often referred to this idea of connecting learning with life in a relational way as "the science of relations."[8] A living education powers the relationship between our children and the authors of what they read, see, and hear in their daily learning rhythm. Our library book choices and curriculum purchases go beyond the question of "What can they learn from this?" to an enquiring notion of "What relationship can they form with this?" A living education that is shaped by the science of relations changes how we help our children learn and begin to form their own new atmospheres and habits.

Charlotte suggests that when a child is born, they are complete and already hold within them all that they are to become (like a seed); they just need the right environment and stimuli to draw their beauty and brilliance out of them! As well as believing this is true, I love that this concept doesn't speak to high achievement or grandiose expectations of our children based on government grading or standardised educational statistics—we can genuinely believe and expect this of every child.

We don't form relationships with facts, lists, and worksheets—we form relationships with people! How we choose our resources and what we present to our children ultimately impacts their connection with the authors and living content. So let's select stories that portray real lives—page-turning tales to talk about well after the schoolbooks have been packed away and as learning leans into play.

Charlotte taught us the power of "telling back" (narration) not only to retain knowledge but as a delicate yet deep method of moulding meaning into our lives from the stories we've read. Over the years I've crafted questions beyond "tell me back" to aid my children's discoveries and connections. As part of our conversations following a read aloud, I invite the children to take a journey with the author, to imagine what their inspiration was, where they got their character ideas, why they might have written it this way. Keep your questions open ended, interesting, and conversational, and watch the wonder unfold.

I would value connection over curriculum every time. Let's build a life and rhythm that leaves room for conversation, disruption, and questions. We all love to finish the chapter, tick all the boxes, and wrap up the day—but did we listen to what our children had to say?

Belief and Books

I remember being around a dinner table with strangers at an awards event when they asked me what my husband would describe as the "we're going to be here all night" question: "So, what do you do?" Over the years I haven't exactly got my answer down to an elevator pitch, but I can easily fill new friends in with a synopsis of my work and passion before my uneaten dessert is assumed finished by the server and without getting on a soapbox! We'd just about covered "Is it legal?" and narrowly avoided the socialisation question before jumping right in with Miss Mason. As the coffee cups were being cleared away and our evening host picked up the microphone to commence the ceremony, the delightful young couple who had graciously endured my impassioned spiel simply said, "So, really it comes down to beliefs and books? That's brilliant!"

I loved their simple novice summary of the Mason way—*belief and books*—but what excites me more is that we are the ones who get to live it out. We get to take it beyond a conversation at a dinner party into the reality of our children's lives, "mind to mind."[9] As we carefully shape the ideas and values that already rule our homes, we begin to change the atmosphere. As we instill habits and rhythms that shape our day, we find discipline of character together. And as we share living ideas with our children, we begin to bring out their best and unique qualities and offer them a life they can truly thrive in.

TAKE A MASON MOMENT:
Suggestions on How to Live Out a Motto That Matters

- Attempt to summarise what "atmosphere, discipline, life" means to you and your family. Write it down, and have it in view to review as you learn and grow.
- Take stock of the atmosphere of your home: observe the sounds, smells, conversation, and values. Note what you celebrate, what you challenge, and how you communicate.
- Have an honest conversation with your spouse or older children about the tone of your relationships in the home, where the pressure points lie, and how you can address them together. Get help from external sources you trust if you need it.
- Change doesn't happen overnight, but if there are changes to be made, choose three areas you can see need work in the atmosphere, write them down, and work towards them slowly, preferably together. Try removing clutter, cultivating conversation around meals, and adding in some classical music to tweak a change in the atmosphere.
- To create a simple rhythm for consistent study, try looping. Loop scheduling is a fancy term I use for arranging my

chosen subjects into an organised list that we can make our way through in any given day or week. I often have a loop for the day (such as mathematics, copy work, reading the Bible) and then a loop for the week. We make our way through the loop, and when we get to the bottom, we just start back at the top again!

- Remember there's no expectation without explanation. Adding a regular pattern or rhythm into a child's life may require repeated explanation, demonstration, and encouragement for motivation. No one responds to "Just do it" (except people who like Nike shoes!).
- Celebrate the wins: enjoy the benefits of an organised bedroom, a finished piece of work, or a tidy pencil tray. I still light a candle to celebrate my clean kitchen!
- Take time to learn what Charlotte meant by "living ideas" beyond just books. What can be brought to life for your children through the mind of another writer or creator?
- Decide who you want to invite to be a guest in your home, whether Shakespeare, David Attenborough, or Anne Frank, and figure out creative ways to introduce them to your children.
- Tell more stories and ask more questions.
- When education is about building relationships and connections, it takes time. Don't rush or try to speed up those "mind to mind" connections—that's down to the child, not you!
- Buy lots of books (or pick them up from the library). You can never go overkill on books if you will actually read them!

Chapter 3

Capturing Attention

No intellectual habit is so valuable as that of attention;
it is a mere habit but it is also the hallmark of an educated person.
CHARLOTTE MASON, *A PHILOSOPHY OF EDUCATION*

Within Charlotte Mason's instructions for education, she emphasised
the power of paying attention, a discipline which is core to her
whole approach. Through the practice of attentiveness, Charlotte
invites us to engage our mind, heart, and soul as we lean in to listen
and learn from the world. It is a habit that we as parents must
first model for our children before we can start to train them
to see that which is worth observing.

The Power of Focused Attention

We live in a world of endless distraction both online and off. Marketers now believe that the most valuable thing they can ever get from you is your attention, so much so that they are paying millions to hold it for as long as possible. There is even a phrase for this tactic, coined by the advertising industry: "the currency of attention." Why is our attention so powerful? Because where we choose to put our attention is where we will ultimately direct our energy and efforts—it is where we will invest our resources and our lives. Where your attention lies, your affections will follow.

I believe we must cultivate the ability to focus our attention in a sustained way on the things that truly matter. This means learning to set aside irrelevant thoughts, to shut out distractions, to be alert to our environment, and to prioritise real-life relationships over social media and entertainment. Living our lives with an awareness of our surroundings, the places we inhabit and visit, and especially the people we come across keeps us present and stops us from missing out on new opportunities for connection and learning. At even a basic level, if a child isn't aware of the importance of paying focused attention where needed, how will they follow an instruction or recognise your voice in an emergency? Paying attention separates the sheep from the goats; it is the difference between the one who reads the application form properly and gets the interview, and the one who manages to fill their name in the incorrect box and gets their application immediately thrown in the bin! Attention not only benefits us academically and creatively; it's also a key to memory making, building intimate relationships, and progressing in one's profession or career.

The habit of attention was so vital to Charlotte that she believed that it would limit the potential of a child if they were not able to master it as a skill and foundation for all types of learning. As Charlotte claimed, "It is impossible to overstate the importance of this habit of attention. It is, to quote words of weight, 'within the reach of every one, and should be made the primary object of all mental discipline'; for whatever the natural gifts of the child, it is only in so far as the habit of attention is cultivated in him that he is able to make use of them."[1]

We can learn so much about the habit of attention from small children, who naturally see what we don't. I remember diligently vacuuming the living room floor to rid my crawling baby of any swallowing opportunity, only to find that they would still uncover the smallest bead that I happened to miss. Children can spot the tiniest of things because they have such a unique perspective. Looking at the world from their level, my children have experienced the world outdoors in a way I no longer can; from finding a dew-dripping spider's web on a spring morning to discovering the tiny froglet hidden in the grasses they were adventuring in. As parents we know we have something to teach our children, but it is also true that they have something to teach us. Children talk and call for our attention a lot, I know. And when weariness overwhelms us, it's easy to say, "In a minute" or "That's wonderful, darling" because we've got our hands in the sink or we're mid-scroll, but when we respond to their attentiveness now, it will solidify this habit for the future.

Capturing the Attention of Young Children

When it comes to younger children, simple little practices that you may already naturally be doing can begin to cultivate and elongate periods of attention. A jigsaw puzzle is fabulous for this; it's a project that is fun to complete and needs to be seen out until the end. When you're down on the carpet finding corners and animal ears to put in place, encourage your child to persist for a little longer if they're tempted to wander off and play with something else. Just a simple "Let's do one more piece" can be enough to finish that chunky twenty-piece animal scene you started together! Before you know it, *one more piece* on the carpet starts to build the resilience needed to complete *one more task* in later life.

LEGOs provide a life lesson for us all. Those small, child-sized pieces of colour that magically create buildings, cars, and worlds can keep young minds (and the young at heart) occupied for hours! But, if your children are prone to always open a new box of toys or treats, just a mere "Let's add some more red blocks to this" could redirect their wandering heart and catch their attention for a few more moments. Charlotte taught that "an observant child should be put in the way of things worth observing,"[2] and I love to use this as a filter for what I expose my children to through their work, rest, and play.

It is fair to say that an overwhelming number of options can be a barrier to a young child's attention when it comes to play. Our children have more choice than ever in their rooms, shelves, and play places. You may like to try minimising choice by rotating boxes and baskets and seeing how long they can focus on what they have in their grasp. As Charlotte reminds us, "It is the mother's part to supplement the child's quick observing faculty with the habit of attention. She must see to it that he does not flit from this to that, but looks long enough at one thing to get a real acquaintance with it."[3]

Bedtime reading can be a simple and beautiful part of the rhythm of a child's life. Yet limiting reading aloud to those sleepy end-of-day moments might minimise your opportunity to strengthen the skill of storytelling. Try reading over breakfast or after nap time. Just five minutes a day of a poem, a short story, or a fable begins to help your children engage with wonderful literature and gets them used to hearing your voice read when they're not falling asleep (hopefully they won't sleep too much over breakfast). Start with shorter readings, and if they're engaging well, lengthen the reading by a few minutes at a time, until they may end up chanting, "Just one more chapter," and you end up having to reheat your morning coffee, again!

Taking baby steps and being patient with the process is key to you and your children finding delight in paying attention until it becomes part of your lives. There's no need to get frustrated or even lord the language of attention over your children. Try to communicate how it would be a "shame to miss out" rather than becoming an imitator of the drill sergeant's straight-backed call of "Atten-TION!"

Stepping Outside to Observe the World

Many people are first introduced to Charlotte Mason because of her emphasis on life outdoors for children. Her many nature-themed quotes and recommendations of journaling have found their way into classrooms, art studios, and homes all around the world. There is no doubt that nature is one of the greatest ways to capture the attention of every child when we choose to see what's often right in front of our eyes.

When my children were much younger, we lived in a small house with a tiny yard, which was edged with beds ready for simple planting. I made good use of those beds to encourage my children outdoors and experimented with small trees, flowers, and even a few vegetables. One of the trees I planted at the bottom of the paved yard was a willow tree, which in hindsight was far too grand for such a small space! Late one winter, as buds were appearing and colourful crocuses began to rear their heads, my son was busy playing near the willow tree when I heard shouts of "Mum, come quick . . ." Now, as a mother of four children, I've learnt that this invitation could mean anything from "There's an airplane in the sky" to "I accidentally poked a stick in my sister's eye and it's bleeding," so I try to respond as quickly as possible! As I approached my son and the young willow tree he was standing by, he pointed out the plethora of ladybirds in every stage of its life cycle all over the leaves of the tree—eggs, larvae, pupae, and adults. He was especially fascinated by the weird-looking larvae that looked nothing like the future adult bugs. Each day that followed, he and his now fully engaged siblings would check in with the ladybirds on the willow tree, until there was nothing more to see.

In Gerald Durrell's book *My Family and Other Animals* we get an inside view of the mind of a child fascinated by the natural world just like my son was. Young Gerald captured and kept magpies, geckos, praying mantises, and many other creatures in a room in the house, whilst observing them daily and making notes on their behaviour to share later with his family. Seeing my own children exploring nature and reading wonderful books like those by Durrell (his Corfu trilogy is incredible), I know how impactful these moments of discovery are and how they are vital to a child's development of attention.

When a child feels that their parents celebrate and reward their moments of active discovery in the world, they are much more likely to stay engaged. It's very natural for parents with a young child to point out what they see around them to the child. I remember taking a walk with one baby in a sling and a tired toddler on the hip, pointing out the cows in the field and the small yellow flowers in the cracks of the wall. We'd stop to listen and point to a cooing dove in the distance.

Our current way of life often makes it seem normal to experience the world through a screen, even from a very young age, but it's up to us to be the seers who point the way outdoors again.

Keeping Attention through Short Lessons

One of Charlotte's tools for encouraging attention in any subject or field of study was to hold short lessons. She argued that "reading lessons must be short; ten minutes or a quarter of an hour of fixed attention is enough for children of the ages we have in view."[4] She held this radical view for most lessons, advocating for it even as children got older, and recent educational research (but unfortunately not mass practice) has shown she was right. Her 1900s ideas relate very closely to modern educator John Medina's *Brain Rules*, where he lays out guidelines for classroom teaching to fully engage the child. Medina states that to keep students engaged, he had to "win the battle for their attention in 10-minute increments."[5]

Charlotte used the language of digestion as a metaphor for learning, directing us to allow children to assimilate ideas before they speak them back to the teacher or educator. John Medina also notes that educators often make the common mistake of "relating too much information, with not enough time devoted to connecting the dots. Lots of force-feeding, very little digestion. This does nothing for the nourishment of the listeners, whose learning is often sacrificed in the name of expediency."[6]

Followers of Charlotte Mason have found these tried-and-true concepts to be fruitful in their child's education, but unfortunately many educators in our traditional school system have not yet recognised their benefits. The author of a recent article in the *Guardian* calls for education reform in light of the global pandemic, encouraging legislators to remember Charlotte and her contemporaries' pioneering work:

Until online learning recently arrived of necessity, the structure of school life also remained as in Victoria's reign. Pupils sit in rows facing a blackboard for one-hour periods— despite Mason's discovery a century ago that 20 minutes is far more effective. They break for Christian festivals and the autumn harvest, without asking whether this makes educational sense. They forget what they have learned and then waste weeks stressfully revising it, before forgetting again. This is a preparation not for life but for obedient monasticism, from which much of school life still derives.[7]

It is ironic that those who often criticise homeschooling as an outdated Victorian idea fail to see the inherent Victorian nature of our public education system! Whilst modern educationalists may want to rethink their reliance on the Victorian practice of sitting in rows like workers in a factory, they may also want to rediscover the age-old value of short lessons. This quote from the *Guardian* reminds us that having a child's obedience and conformity is not the same as having a child's attention. Quiet compliance is not the same as deep engagement.

Consuming information is not the equivalent of real knowledge and wisdom.

The privilege of homeschooling is that you can structure your day around your children's needs to help keep their attention sharp. Mornings might be for focused time, and afternoons for more free pursuits. You may want to try a shorter lesson if you find your child lacks attention and gets fidgety after a certain period, if they "can't remember" when asked for feedback, or if they constantly ask for water, snacks, a trip to the toilet, or even *world peace* rather than do the work! Short lessons help us assimilate knowledge in small sections, and this kind of appetising, rich feast of learning helps us stay satiated long after the lesson has ended.

Paying Attention to Your Child

I first realised I was likely nearsighted whilst working late in the college library trying to finish a written assignment. I had been staring down at my handwriting moving its way across the page for so much time that when I glanced up at the library clock to check the time, everything went blurred and out of focus. Looking at something close in front of us for a long time, whether physical or emotional, can leave us tunnel visioned, blurry eyed, and unable to adjust to the wide view.

If we are honest, we can sometimes be shortsighted about our own children. We may focus so much on the daily tasks—completing the math worksheet, learning to tell nouns from verbs—that we fail to see the bigger picture of who our children are and where their interests are leading them. But we need to pay attention to our children before they will pay attention to us.

I remember coaching a young mother who had three lively sons, all under the age of six. One of her questions was "How do I even start to help them with the habit of attention when they're on the move all the time?" We all know children love being on the move; being active and lively is part of childhood. Some personalities just need more movement than others! You have to remember that we are working *with* our children and not against them. Social media advice and blog inspiration, albeit well meaning, is often generalised, sometimes idealistic, and rarely bespoke. At the end of the day, you know your children best, and you are the best mother for them.

Whenever I am coaching a mother using Charlotte Mason's ideas, I often start by recommending a period of observation to jot a few notes down about each child. This may sound over the top as you're with them all day every day, but it's helpful to reflect on what makes them a unique individual—for example, what topics draw their attention, who they admire, what their personality is like, what you suspect their preferred learning style is, and what they love to do.[8] All children pay attention to something, but it's usually led by desire, curiosity, or entertainment value. Mastering their motivation is key. Our role as educators is to divert them into something new rather than just distract them from something old.

Once you've spent time observing and taking notes for each child (this might be over a period of a few weeks), you will have a baseline understanding of your child—both their strengths and weaknesses. You can draw out who they already are and redirect where necessary to strengthen them in important life skills. Mothers report to me that when they help their children strengthen the habit of attention, the children can stay with new ideas for longer and make better use of the knowledge or experience they have encountered.

Remember you are the first person that your child will likely fix their attention on. The power of the parent or prominent adult in a child's life is paramount to their development. They are constantly observing your habitual expressions of kindness and loving investment of time. If we're anxiously trying to *habit train* our children and it results in irritability, impatience, and a busy mind, then we miss the opportunity to build true, rich, and lasting relationships with our children. The challenge with home education is that the lines between being the parent and the educator are often blurred; when asked to choose between the two, I always say be a mother first. What if the loving expression of your motherhood is the greatest lesson your child can ever learn from you?

At the end of the day our children will pay attention to what we observe ourselves. They will respond to how we fix our gaze and how we are amazed by nature, by story, and by sound. This beautiful and generous habit develops with the child: as they look, they will be rewarded; as they listen, they will grow. And it doesn't stop when they are no longer young. As a mother of an adult and teenagers, I'm learning that their late-night desire to unload or just reflect is as important as listening to my toddler's midday chatter. Our listening ear endorses their voice and what they've paid attention to that day. We applaud them for having an opinion, provide a place to speak out, and give them a chance to leave the worries of the day behind. I keep my attention on them so that they keep their attention on what matters.

TAKE A MASON MOMENT:
Suggestions for Capturing Attention

- It starts with you—pause on one thing, wherever possible.
- Pause and pay attention to your senses when outdoors. What can you see, smell, touch, hear (and taste where it's safe to do so) from where you're standing? Encourage your children to do the same.
- Ask open-ended, interesting questions about a beautiful art scene, a story, or a natural situation, such as "Where do you think that road leads?" or "What would you have done in that situation?"

- Listen to music intentionally; be alert for instruments, phrases, or themes that you can share with children.
- Read poetry out loud with a pre-explained listening mission. Listen for a favourite word, phrase, or sentence. Encourage children to picture the words in their mind.
- When a child is tempted to give up on a book, game, or task quite quickly, say, "Just one more minute" and set a timer. Stretch it to two minutes next time.
- If your child is struggling to recollect, hold attention, and/or narrate when reading, read shorter passages.
- When visiting an art gallery or museum, encourage children to find one brilliant piece or picture to tell you about at the end. Don't expect them to pay attention to the whole exhibit. If they seem to be getting bored, ask, "Have you found your 'one' yet?"
- Pick a daily outdoor observation rhythm and have an allocated notebook to write down what you see. This could be cloud shapes, leaf colours, temperature, weather, etc. Focus on one for six weeks or so; do this daily and enjoy the progression.
- Encourage your children's questions; they reflect engagement and attention. Write them down, even if you can't answer straight away—foster questions about people, books, art, politics, theology, etc. Don't be afraid of them, don't dismiss them; embrace your children's curiosity!
- Put your phone down.

Chapter 4

Standing Back

Let children alone. . . . the education of habit is successful in so far as it enables the mother to let her children alone, not teasing them with perpetual commands and directions—a running fire of Do and Don't; but letting them go their own way and grow, having first secured that they will go the right way, and grow to fruitful purpose.

CHARLOTTE MASON, *HOME EDUCATION*

Charlotte Mason encouraged parents to stand back, allowing the processes of childhood and education to do their natural work without unnecessary interruptions and overwork on behalf of the parent. Within the home education philosophy, this is known as "masterly inactivity."[1]

Learning to Let Go

Charlotte argued that we should "let children alone," within an environment that ensures they will not go astray. This notion, known as *masterly inactivity*, is by no means an excuse to walk away from our parental responsibility. It doesn't negate our involvement or mean we can fully delegate our responsibility to ensure our children "receive" an education. In fact, it's quite the opposite. Masterly inactivity offers the opportunity for intentional thought, planning, and guidance on the part of the parent, whilst allowing children the freedom to learn and explore for themselves.

When a young mother had just given birth to her second child via C-section and needed some support, my eldest daughter and a few of her friends rose to the occasion and took a sweet little two-year-old boy in for a day or two by turn. This opportunity bestowed upon our household the surprising realisation that we'd forgotten what it's like to have a young toddler around the house! It also gave me a fresh way to understand masterly inactivity. As the boy was tottering around my kitchen in the morning, I noticed that he was making a determined beeline for our dog's food bowl. Aside from a few leftover biscuits, the only potential threat to him (or my kitchen floor) was that the bowl was full of fresh water. I decided that rather than throw out a gentle but stern no, I would lightheartedly put my future grandparent hat on and watch how it might play out.

Barefoot and curious, Ben began by dipping his toe in the water bowl, followed by his whole foot, which of course made the water start to splash out.

"Wow, that's amazing," I quietly muttered whilst eagerly awaiting his next move.

His foot washing was seamlessly followed by him picking up the whole bowl and pouring the contents all over my kitchen floor. He finished his brief adventure by dancing in the water, splashing like Gene Kelly singing in the rain without an ounce of concern or regret. At that point I saw water slowly trickling towards the kitchen cupboards and thought I'd better get involved.

"Hey, Ben, this looks like so much fun, but I think we may need to clean up now. Can you find the mop?" I asked.

We both spotted a mop and bucket in the corner of the kitchen. Much to his disappointment, I made it to the mop first, but we shared the clean-up job like two old friends waltzing in the kitchen together. My hands were high up on the mop handle, his were lower down towards the floor, as we finished the work and made a memory from a moment.

This story is a simplistic illustration of the concept of masterly inactivity told via an accidental puddle in my kitchen. Our little friend had discovered something new and wanted to engage. Rather than push him into it, or even away from it, I had left him room and time to figure out the possibilities from a safe distance. If I hadn't held back, then we never would have created the moment of magic together. I left him alone, but I was still there to help, support, and clean up afterwards!

Laying Out a Feast of Learning

Just like Miss Mason, I love a good food analogy! I want you to imagine cooking a meal and then laying out each dish on a beautifully set table for your family to enjoy. As they each sit down and prepare to eat, something unusual happens. Instead of letting people dig in, you begin to spoon each dish into their mouths, describing what each flavour will taste like, what texture they should feel, and how the taste will melt away. You follow this up by confirming how each dish will make them feel afterwards, deciding for them whether they will like it or not. Let's be honest, what at first may seem like comfort and convenience will soon start to feel like control! Funnily enough, this strange picture depicts what many traditional education models end up becoming whether they intend it or not. Learning becomes an outside-in experience, where the educator spoon-feeds the learner empty facts that might stick in the mouth but never in the mind.

Now I want you to picture preparing another meal for your family. The table is laid out in the same beautiful, welcoming way. Yet this time as everyone sits down, you throw your napkin on your knee and say, "Dig in, enjoy, and let me know what you think." As everyone around the table eagerly responds to your invitation, you hear the satisfying sounds of enjoyment from those who are experiencing culinary bliss. As the meal carries on there is an awareness of some children leaving certain dishes for later or expressing their delight about something they have discovered. Collective and collaborative conversation flows from all sides with phrases such as "This reminds me of" or "I want to try making this for myself" or even "Try this one with that, it tastes incredible." It is rare that you need to remind your family of their hunger when the feast before them is so inviting.

The difference here is so key to our understanding of this concept of masterly inactivity. In both examples of the meal, we are the ones preparing and offering a table of possibilities to our family. But the difference is in how much we as the parent trust in what we have prepared and how much we trust in our children to respond. When it comes to teaching and learning, we so often cook up a feast of learning and then try to either force-feed it to our children or resort to eating it for them!

Charlotte believed that parents "should give their children the ease of a good deal of letting alone, and should not oppress the young people with their own anxious care."[2] For a living education to take root in a child's life, they must be left to ruminate, reflect on, and retell all they have learnt. This position of parent/teacher is quite countercultural to our usual lecturer-expert style of teaching and takes desire and intentional action on our part. This is ultimately an inside-out education. It challenges how we view a child; it beckons us to believe that they are already whole; our job is to then facilitate variety and quality of study through books, experiences, and activities whilst leaving room for inside-out processing rather than outside-in spoon-feeding.

Leaving Them Alone to Learn

In his book *Raising Children: Surprising Insights from Other Cultures*, anthropologist David F. Lancy opens the introduction with the subtitle *Leave the Kids Alone*. Rather than being a rehash of the lyric (that did pop into my head) from the 1979 Pink Floyd hit "Another Brick in the Wall," Lancy's title was in fact a reference to a powerful takeaway from his research regarding different societies around the world. Here is a glimpse of his observation about the Maniq society who reside in southern Thailand:

> While there is no coercion (the Maniq believe that trying to shape the child's behavior will make him/her ill) and no "curriculum," children effectively manage their own "education." Indeed, there are no words in their language for *teaching* or *learning*. Children become fully competent in the adult repertoire of skills by fourteen, including the ability to independently navigate and exploit the forest's resources.[3]

The idea that there is no literal word for *teaching* in this unique culture fascinates me as it shows how much the Maniq must integrate learning into every aspect of life. From an anthropological perspective we can see that children will naturally learn, explore, reach out, ask questions, and master any necessary repertoire of skills when they see the need for them. One fascinating fact about the Maniq people is that they give children their own tools to use from about the age of three! This is a great example of what happens when a culture expects the child to become a contributor to the community from a young age. Children develop competencies quickly when parents raise expectations and don't always do tasks for them. We may not need to give more tools to our children, but we can put more power in their hands.

In their journal article "'We Don't Allow Children to Climb Trees': How a Focus on Safety Affects Norwegian Children's Play in Early-Childhood Education and Care Settings," researchers Sandseter and Sando note how bureaucracy is creeping into playful education systems like Norway, which have previously been renowned for their positive approach to risk taking. Some Norwegian schools have now added into their guidance that "climbing in trees is accepted but only up to a certain height and always with adult supervision."[4] I am certain that the older generation who used to fall out of trees and brush themselves off would balk at such a restrictive approach to this age-old pastime. We must ask ourselves, Why does everything have to be done in half measures with adult supervision? The researchers note that engaging in risky activities, such as swinging from trees or jumping from high places, provides a child an opportunity to understand boundaries and overcome perilous situations. By expressing curiosity and excitement, and by taking part in "risky play," they are in fact rehearsing for real-life scenarios down the line in which they must weigh potential risks and benefits before acting.

A measure of risk taking is an important part of helping children become more resilient learners. Despite our desire to give a child the freedom to grow, our predisposition for red tape as a society means we now put warning signs up where common sense used to prevail. We are more educated, informed, and aware of potential dangers than ever before. Yet I'm sometimes afraid that our status as guardians and protectors can veer into overprotecting their minds and intellect from the wild places too! Childhood is not meant to be a sanitised programme dictated and designed by adults.

As an aside, I think we have not just homogenised play in the name of safety, but we have narrowed the options of what play can look like altogether in the pursuit of comfort and entertainment. Children are naturally curious and are inclined to discover, touch, climb, and reach out into the unknown. The simplest and most natural of stimuli can keep them intrigued for long periods of time. Whenever young children come over to our home, I love to grab our ready-made boxes of shells, beach treasures, and pine cones for them to hold and explore new imaginary games with. I often wonder if we're in danger of over-entertaining a generation when the natural world is already set up to provoke awe and wonder.

Leaving them alone to learn, whether indoors or outside, is not about making it easier for our children; in fact, it is about adding a unique element of challenge. If we try to do it for them all the time or never expose them to any difficulty, whether on a playground or on a page, we basically end up raising children without intellectual resilience.

Learning to Trust the Process

Charlotte's guidance to "let the children alone" helps us set the tone for our children's learning experience. Her writings, particularly in her book *School Education*, give many practical applications around masterly inactivity and how it shows itself in children's play, work, friendships, and even how they spend their pocket money. Charlotte writes about the importance of children forming their own opinions and having freedom to be spontaneous in life. Parents and educators can have the power to act, but also the strength to hold back. We can achieve the delicate balance of knowing when to step in and when to step away.

Through the Wordsworth poem "Expostulation and Reply" Charlotte found great insight into the concept of masterly inactivity. The poem centres around a conversation between a younger version of Wordsworth and a schoolmaster as they debate whether learning can happen beyond just the schoolroom. Wordsworth argues that by sitting alone in nature, in a state of "wise passiveness," he is able to feed his soul and find a type of inspiration that cannot be found in a textbook. Only by adopting a position of active waiting or being proactively passive can we open ourselves up to new types of learning. Nature observation particularly requires much patience; the best results come from being quietly present. There are times when I have personally sat in a wooded area or perched by the water's edge and seen the most beautiful birds and wildlife. A moment later or with the usual hurry to get home after a walk, I would have missed the heron standing on the bank of the river, and the green finches gathered in the park bushes.

Charlotte believed that practicing masterly inactivity gives agency to the child and shows grace and confidence in the parent, but perhaps above all else, it is an exercise in trust.

The phrase *helicopter parenting* speaks of mothers or fathers who constantly hover above their children and involve themselves intrusively and detrimentally in every aspect of their lives. The parents' constant supervision as the children grow up eliminates any chance of healthy boundaries between them. This is the type of parent who not only does everything for their children but fights their battles for them as well. If you add the homeschooling dynamic into this equation, the children can end up with an upbringing where it is all laid out on a plate and the teacher becomes a dictator because it is easier to keep a tight rein on their children's activity. Parents who take this approach may have external compliance from their children but still be in danger of losing the internal battle. We end up raising children who play it too safe, rarely think for themselves, and don't even know how to fail.

When we find ourselves locked into *helicopter homeschooling*, we must admit that we have lost trust in ourselves and our children. In the tiny green book *Charlotte Mason Reviewed*, Jenny King reflects on the challenging process of masterly inactivity, saying that it "is hard to achieve because the grown-ups are so anxious for the children to have everything and miss nothing."[5] We must take a step back from what we think we should be doing and start again from a place of confident trust and wise passiveness.

The practice of masterly inactivity is not about refusing to help your children; the intersection of motherhood, childhood, and education comes into play here. Relationship over results is the key to lowering stress and creating a hospitable learning environment. It is not an excuse for apathy, justification for leaving children unsupervised, or a chance to take your foot off the parenting pedal. Masterly inactivity is fully about trusting the child, yourself, and the tried and tested methods. Day by day it may look like not jumping to answer their questions for them and allowing the "penny to drop" as they figure it out (or research it) themselves. It's about leaving space for problem solving and conversation cultivating wherever possible. It's about allowing our children to push their own boundaries, make their own observations, and build confidence to freely share their opinion.

I've spoken to so many parents over the years who have started a journey with Charlotte Mason but have faltered because the tools and methods felt far too simplistic and they weren't seeing immediate results. But this is where we must trust masterly inactivity and the understanding of the inner processes of education. Where traditional educational methods may produce immediate results—as shown through a child's right answers on tests and completed directives—Charlotte's guidance creates long-term, deeply rooted formation of thoughts and ideas. Whilst not producing immediate, visible "results," her methods create a lifelong learner over time.

When a familiar concern from homeschooling parents is "Am I doing enough?" it can in turn raise the possibility that their child is going to get "behind" in some shape or form. Yet if we choose to educate our children from home, we give them an even greater opportunity to run their own race, and if this is so, how could they possibly get "behind" anyone? By what standard are we judging? The norms of standardised testing, marks, and grades from the school classroom overcrowd our minds. We need to ensure our children are fixed on their own path rather than beginning the comparison game so early in life. In homeschooling, we get to set our own benchmarks.

Through Charlotte's philosophical approach, children will have exposure to great books, thinkers, and creators. They will take time to enjoy the great outdoors and have adults in their lives to process their thoughts with. Charlotte taught us that "self-education is the only possible education; the rest is mere veneer laid on the surface of a child's nature."[6] When you cut through the six volumes of books, myriads of *Parents' Review* articles, as well as her own creative devotional writings, Charlotte's ideas were ultimately quite simple: it was all about helping children become receptive individuals capable of self-education.

Learning to Trust the Child

I always love it whenever my friend comes over with her children to play in the park which wraps around our house, especially during the summertime. I enjoy brewing a pot of coffee, then grabbing a blanket and a couple of mugs before sitting down to watch our children play. They run with the dog, build dens in the trees, and beg for cold drinks or ice creams whenever the opportunity arises! Watching them often reminds me of my own childhood summers riding bikes and climbing trees, and I always look on with immense gratitude. There's something so endearing about watching your children as they freely navigate the world and flourish whilst we cheer them on from the sidelines. Perhaps this should be our aim for their educational life as well as their social life. Charlotte encouraged us to take an overseeing-whilst-standing-back approach by reminding us that we know our children better than others do, and for that reason we should believe in them more!

Trusting the child is foundational to our growth and development as a parent/educator. The more familiar we are with Charlotte's ideas, the more we'll trust they will help our children thrive. That's why it's important to continue to learn and read for ourselves about the *why* as well as the *how*. This trust starts with Charlotte's first principle "Children are born persons." This approach to education always challenges our view of children and their ability to connect with the world around them. Do we believe that they are whole and ready for the world, or do we feel the responsibility to fill them?

Charlotte encouraged parents to be secure in who they are by showing not only confidence in themselves but confidence in their children;

stating that this was fundamental to masterly inactivity. We can be confident that our children's knowledge and skills, as well as their character and values, are being formed every day by the bountiful feast we lay before them. It's incredible that we have that front-row seat on observing their connections with the world when they are young and get to see the fascinating inner workings of their young minds. After all, the cliché is true that if we don't believe in our children, we cannot expect them to believe in themselves. Yet this concept so often starts with believing in ourselves first.

Learning to Trust Yourself

Even after only two decades of parenting, I have witnessed many books, fads, and so-called "experts" come in and out of the conversation on raising children. The rise and fall of these voices often comes out of a desperation for parents, especially in the Western world, to grapple with answers, steps, and support to do the seemingly impossible task of raising humans. We ask for opinions from strangers on the internet and then wonder why their solutions didn't quite work out for our context. We can so quickly lose confidence in our own ability to nurture, and begin to consider others the experts on our children, even about the simplest of things.

Parents can often create barriers to home educating their children because they feel they are not clever or academic enough. I'm not sure what your own educational history was or how you responded to the learning environment you were brought up in, but we all had to start somewhere. One of the earliest pieces of advice I received about home-schooling was that you only need to be a few days ahead of your children's learning. This has proven to be true, but I have also learnt that we can walk *alongside* our children in the subjects we are unfamiliar with and share the journey with them. The emphasis isn't on how much we as the parents know and can pass on, it is about believing that we are the ones to cultivate space that allows our children to learn. I haven't always found this easy; the freedom to trust myself whilst carrying responsibility and accountability for my children's education has been a journey.

Charlotte said, "Parents should trust themselves more."[7] You don't need a master's degree in education to understand your own children. We are the ones to set our children up to win, to thrive, and to grow into who they were created to be. You are the best parent for your child. I was, however, really tested on this idea with my youngest child, even after being a home educator for many years. She took longer to read than her older siblings even though her foundations and beginnings were much like those of my older children. In her short lifetime she'd heard powerful stories, constant verse, and rhyme, and she'd spent hours and hours outdoors. This young girl was alert, vibrant, and bright, but the decoding of words on a page simply did not click with her.

I wasn't concerned about it at first, until a few negative comments drifted our way, with people starting to suggest possible learning difficulties due to her being *behind*.

One day my living room was brimming with children, snacks, and board games; one of my daughters was as usual at the heart of the party and got the game started. This particular game required the reading of cards for instructions, and not quite fluent in this skill, she asked her brother to help her. I was in the kitchen but still in full earshot of the dialogue that ensued:

Friends: "Ha ha, [my daughter's name] can't read."

(I'm biting my tongue in the next room.)

My daughter: "I can read, I just don't know all the words yet."

These occasional instances caused my usual steadfastness in the methods to begin to wobble. My daughter was confident and happy at her pace; the problem was not in her but in me. I had to remind myself of Charlotte's words—to be wise and purposeful in allowing my daughter's natural learning processes to take place, and celebrate the gifts, skills, and habits she was shining in.

You'll be pleased to know the story ends well. We stayed consistent and made delight a priority in her reading. Soon enough, the day came when reading, as we say in our house, "just clicked." Before long she was devouring chapter books and biographies and became the leader of every board game she was invited to join. As we grow and continue in our own learning journey, we will gradually understand (and relearn) the powerful capabilities of our own minds, as well as our children's. Like all the best things in life, slow growth is strong growth, and in this process, we learn to trust, over and over again. Will you be strong enough to stand back?

TAKE A MASON MOMENT:
Suggestions for Standing Back

- Read and absorb as much of Charlotte Mason's original writings on education as you can to grow your own understanding. As your understanding grows, so does your trust. It is not just about knowing the tasks; it is about trusting the truth.
- Prepare environments, resources, and short lessons that allow children to take as much ownership of their learning as possible.
- Invest in your own learning and play. Charlotte tells us it's the secret sauce to practising masterly inactivity.
- Pause before you pounce—what you deem as a "wrong answer" is sometimes a journey towards a brilliant idea or a rich educational connection.

- Cultivate an understanding and compassion for the child's stage of learning, rather than comparing them to a system's expectations.
- Stop doing it for them. Observe yourself and how you teach your children. At what point do you allow them or yourself to give in too easily? Feel the stretch a little.
- Relax and enjoy your learning days—laugh together, dream together, experience wonder together. Keep childhood at the forefront, not curriculum.
- Practise active listening from when your children are young. The toddler chatter soon becomes connections and narrations.
- Make a plan but stay flexible.
- Encourage questions, and equip your children to find out the answers.
- Stock your home library with great books, then let your children pick books from your shelves. Give them agency over their reading for enjoyment and fun.
- Keep a journal of verbal connections, overheard comments, cool questions, and interesting narrations. Look back at it and reflect. Remind yourself you're doing a great job; you should trust yourself more!

Part 2

Reframing Education

Chapter 5

Masters of Narration

This, of telling again, sounds very simple but it is really a magical creative process by means of which the narrator sees what he has conceived, so definite and so impressive is the act of narrating that which has been read only once.

CHARLOTTE MASON, *A PHILOSOPHY OF EDUCATION*

Charlotte Mason showed us how through the art of telling back the things we learn, our knowledge of people, places, paintings, and poetry becomes a part of who we are. As parents and educators, we can use narration to build connections and deepen relationships whilst making stories come alive through our children's retelling.

Discovering the Art of Telling Back

I secretly love to hear the sound of feet bounding downstairs as my teenage sons come to join me in the kitchen, especially when they stop to talk about a book or something they are learning. By now we know the drill: I pop the kettle on, and one of my sons hops on the kitchen counter, ready for his brew. On one specific occasion, my son had been lost in his room reading *The Monk Who Shook the World*, which is Cyril Davey's biography of Martin Luther. I poured two hot, steaming mugs and said words that have opened so many doors for us: "So tell me about what you've been reading." And by retelling monk stories between sips of tea, we recreate a familiar scene that has been an active part of his educational life since he was six years old.

"Narration" is the simple practice of telling back what we've heard, seen, or experienced for the purpose of solidifying meaning, taking ownership, and improving retention of the material. Young children first express themselves orally and later progress to writing compositions inspired by readings and experiences. I love the way Charlotte described this tool: "Narrating is an *art*, like poetry-making or painting, because it is *there*, in every child's mind, waiting to be discovered, and is not the result of any process of disciplinary education."[1]

Narration is one of the most powerful tools we have infused into our family culture. The practice of *telling back* has found a rightful place in the rhythm of our learning days, forming beautiful fruit in my children day after day. There is beauty in the sound of a story being told again.

It is a well-published theory that when we receive information through lectures or reading, we remember only about 5–10 percent of what we learnt after a short period of time. Yet when we teach that same knowledge to others, we retain up to 90 percent simply because sharing with others always highlights fresh relevance.[2] This is perhaps one reason home educators often say their real education began when they started teaching their children, but also explains why narration works so well in practice.

I have rarely used the word *narration* in my instruction over the years, yet we embed the practice of it into all our lessons and subjects. The teacher-parent provides the stimulus with one perfectly timed question, opening the door for a rich retelling of a historic tale, an epic journey, or a classic piece of art. Through the creative process of narration, the seeds of storytelling produce a fruit of emotional, oral, and educational literacy in our children.

Charlotte describes narration as a form of mental digestion. Just as food fuels the body, knowledge provides nutrients for the mind. Dry facts and information hold little long-term value, but living ideas followed by narration become part of us. With no red pen in hand or explanatory lectures at the ready, we are to "let the children alone." The educator stands back and allows the child to form a connection with what they're reading or experiencing, giving room for the child to express findings in their own words.

I've been fortunate enough to instill this habit into my children from the early years of their education. My understanding of narration grew after quiet readings of *Miracles on Maple Hill* and *The Trumpet of the Swan*. My children's responses to these two books brought joy and depth to our conversation around the table. And yet, narration is not limited to only reading. We slowly learnt how to incorporate the art of telling back into our study of paintings, literature, music, nature, and history.

I sometimes hear from many struggling homeschooling mothers who have introduced this concept later in childhood. They send messages asking for help, as they can't get their son or daughter to tell back. This is often because they think a retelling should look a certain way or tick a certain box. Fortunately, narration doesn't have to be the same with every child; they are born persons, beautifully individual and ready to reveal what's already inside them in their own unique way.

Catching Narration Early

Apart from a child taking their first steps, there is perhaps no greater thrill for a parent than when that child begins to talk. There is often excitement and a little overzealous interpretation whilst waiting for them to speak their first words. Whether it is uttering Mama, Dada, or announcing a full-on sonnet, we love to predict how their childhood babblings will foreshadow their future oratory success.

I fondly remember the day when one of my sons desperately tried to tell his big sister and me that he wanted to watch "kinawin." "Kinawin, kinawin, kinawin," he repeated, getting more frustrated each time we failed to understand what he was talking about. Eventually we said to him, "Show us what you mean," and he took my hand, confidently leading me to a picture book with a penguin on the front! A *kinawin* was a penguin in his world.

This sweet boy had wanted to watch a cartoon he loved with a penguin in it, and we secretly hoped he would never learn the correct pronunciation. My grown-up language just wasn't in tune with his childlike wonder. That day I squeezed my son tightly and apologized for the delay as we sat and watched his kinawin show. Sometimes we think children have a communication problem, when it is in fact we who have an issue with interpretation. Children have a strong desire to communicate about things they love. The secret of narration is to interpret what they love and let them talk about it.

Charlotte expressed that children have an innate desire to recount the adventures, sightings, and scenes in their mind. As she puts it, "He tells everything with splendid vigour in the true epic vein."[3] They want to explain about the dog they saw in the park, the bug in Grandma's garden, or the ice cream cone that melted down their hand. It's natural for children to report on their lives in a way that makes memories and creates conversation within the context of relationships. If we want to let them learn, we must nurture this desire to talk.

We may be tempted to block out childlike chatterings or nod obliviously as we attend to the more important business at hand. Whilst I'm not saying our children must always have our complete and undivided attention, it is vital to acknowledge them when they share with us what they love. Listening to them gives value to their voice at a young age and gives them a foundation for storing relevant knowledge. Even before we expect a formal narrative response after a story or observation, we are training our hearts and theirs to tune in and learn to respect the teller and the told.

Narrating Living Books

I'm continuously amazed by the questions and ideas that emerge from narrating the living books, stories, pictures, sights, and sounds that fill our day. I've discovered, studied, and relished the fruit of my children retelling a story in their own words. I've marveled at the fact that by allowing them to assimilate and regurgitate the connections in their own, individual way, they form a relationship with the subject. Narration is one of the most powerful tools in our homeschool tool kit, but you can easily master it whether you home educate or not.

The art and practice of narration is intrinsically linked with the use of living books. Although we have a whole chapter in this book dedicated to delving deeper into the subject of living books, it is worth reminding ourselves here that a living book is generally one written by a passionate author who then attempts to communicate this enthusiasm within the first few pages of their book. A child should be able to "tell back" from a living book, and you can determine this for yourself by reading a short section. Read a paragraph of a book, put the book down, and then try to communicate what the paragraph contained to another person. Or try the one-page test: open a book and read it aloud for yourself. Does it draw you in? Does it interest you? Does it leave you wanting to read on? If it doesn't, then be brave enough to put the book down and move on.

It may seem harsh to move on without persevering too long, but once you find the books that hook your children, you yourself will be hooked. We only have so much time with our children in these fleeting days, so there is no point in flogging a dead book. Whether it is through making a connection with the English knights of old or finding life lessons in fairy tales and Aesop's fables, you will soon start to fill their treasure-trove minds with the same pieces that caught your attention.

Charlotte likens the use of lecturing on information without a personal connection to teaching a child a floating, idle song which drifts out as lightly as it goes in. When we give our children the opportunity to get in touch with a living book, however, we are handing them a spade and allowing them to "dig their knowledge, of whatever subject, for themselves out of the fit book."[4] What a child has to dig for becomes their possession.

We may be learned in the ways of a Charlotte Mason-led approach, but until we consistently practise reading living books and hearing our children narrate them back, we will never fully experience the elation of intimate connection it can bring.

Narrating to Make Personal Connections

One goal of narration is to make natural connections. I love to think of learning as a giant paper chain. Each person from history is a link our children can visit through what they read, hear, or see; each new insight is like one of those decorative slips of paper edged with glue, with the possibility of connecting to another ready to be hung in celebration.

Narration offers a truly connected experience—an opportunity for our children to lock in to what they're hearing and build a relationship with history, lives, and language. How incredible that we're not merely training our children to remember lists and dates and facts; we're inviting them to be part of the story.

The ideas and images that our children store in their minds are often expressed in the most delightful ways. An early homeschool memory is hearing one of my children make a connection between the biblical account of Moses as a baby and the 1784 folk song "Bye, Baby Bunting," in which the picture book illustration showed Baby Bunting in a basket (just like Moses, of course). I remember my youngest son pointing to a landscape whilst walking in the English countryside and exclaiming that it looked like a Constable painting. In that revelatory moment of delight (for me and him), I realised that I could never force, coax, or create a reaction like that from my child. It's all their doing, and that's why we "let them alone." It is this ability to link people, places, paintings, and poetry from seemingly disconnected patterns that makes this type of learning so special.

A few years ago, my children and I were reading Shakespeare's *Hamlet*. I spent time with them looking at Gertrude's speech describing the tragic death of Ophelia. The mention of water, willows, and wildflowers prompted an inspired connection to our local park. So we took the book with us and walked across the green field towards the park. Approaching the river, we wanted to not quite reenact the scene, but to imagine what it may have looked like. The swinging, swaying willows dangled over the water within reach of "weedy trophies" such as daisies, columbine, and violets mentioned in the script. We were delightfully dramatic, flinging our arms and picturing the scene whilst reading the words; we imagined the floating, mermaid-like dress trailing across the water as Ophelia still had a grasp of her wildflowers. The iconic words of a world-class communicator connected beautifully with our daily nature walk in a park. Over four hundred years after the words were originally written, Shakespeare had come alive again under a willow tree.

Narrating with a Playful Spirit

Narration is not limited to written or oral mediums; we can even introduce narration through play. As Heraclitus, an ancient Greek philosopher, once pondered, "Time is a game played beautifully by children." As our homeschool journey unfolded over time, I noticed that my children began retelling the stories and poems we'd read through their play. I suddenly realised they were taking what we had shared in our formal time and translating it into their free time. I've learnt that leaving space for young children to express themselves through their innate, playful creativity and imagination is vital for the embedding of knowledge and ideas. We can teach our children to play as a response to learning—not just as a break from it.

Children naturally want to bring stories to life. Encouraging our children to reenact what they are learning in dramatic form can result in their deeper curiosity about the subject—followed by additional reenactments! I have personally observed my children act out everything from battles in Narnia to the wonder of the Nativity story. These living room productions played through pulled-out toy boxes and strewn-out dressing-up stashes help our children to form key, albeit sometimes whimsical, connections with literary characters and history.

Charlotte suggests we should allow our children to play out their interpretation of their readings, and in doing so they will develop "capacity, character, countenance, initiative and a sense of responsibility."[5] When we allow play as a response to educational input, we learn to trust the process of feeding our children a wonderful feast of literature and life. Play helps children enter the story for themselves.

Narrating to Build Relationships

Asking great questions is the foundation of great narration and the soil for growing stronger relationships with children. Questions unlock learning but also deepen relational connections. I fondly remember the early years of establishing the habit of narration in our family. I loved being creative in my requests after reading or observing, mixing things up with queries such as "How would you have responded in that situation?" or "How do you think the artist was feeling?" Or I would use gentler nudges such as "What happened next?"

I have learnt that being creative with questioning allows children to be creative with their retelling. Changing my style, tone, and type of request kept my children on their toes, paying attention and wondering how we were going to begin our time of telling back. As much as my children were eagerly anticipating my prompts, I was anticipating their wonderful responses. Speaking and listening create intimacy and deepen familial bonds.

Even when we take a break from formal learning, the power of narration still remains. There are days when an off-the-cuff table conversation prompts me to grab more books from the shelves as we recall what "that reminds me of." As we informally build relationships, we capture moments when our children voice their narrations alone, with no help from us. The lines between mother and educator can be beautifully blurred when both roles are built on a foundation of relationship.

As we introduce and teach narration, sometimes we must learn to wait. Our anticipation of grand conversations and connections can take time, and the magic doesn't happen every time. If we approach narration as a journey, as a lifelong learning opportunity that strengthens and develops through consistency, enthusiasm, and example, we will be free of the pressure to "make it happen" for our children.

Unlike studying for an exam, the outcome of narration can be hard to tangibly measure at first. We're not awarding our children with certificates and sticker charts; we're not coaxing comprehension answers out of them and marking their efforts with ticks and stars. We're reading and interacting with great minds and patiently waiting for unique outcomes, as any great curator does. By establishing rhythms where our children can grow roots of attention, observation, and application, we plant them in a wider space.

Charlotte believed that the ultimate goal of the early years was "to show that the chief function of the child—his business in the world during the first six or seven years of his life—is to find out all he can, about whatever comes under his notice, by means of his five senses."[6] As we encourage our children to narrate their learning, they often begin to engage with their whole selves, adding movement and imitation after hearing stories and seeing art. As we let them alone, we find our children copying statues with their bodies to mimic Degas's ballerinas. They walk nobly like a king as Elgar's "Pomp and Circumstance" plays on the radio. They cross the characters of Greek heroes with Bible characters and liken books about Holocaust survivors to Shakespeare's medieval tales. Children use retelling as a means to keep stories and knowledge digestible for life.

And as the children narrate, they continue to grow. As their bodies become taller, their dialogue becomes deeper, and their ideas become much grander than before. We as mothers are reminded once more that with every story read, every skill mastered, every hour spent planning, our investment is always worthwhile. As the stories of our children's lives unfold, we wait expectantly for the next opportunity to put the kettle on, pull up a chair, and listen to our child recount what they have learnt.

TAKE A MASON MOMENT:
Suggestions for Mastering Narration

- Listen to your children's "important" talk and chatter when they are young. We can choose to be attentive to our children's observations before the formal schooling years by writing them down.
- Create a rhythm of reading aloud to your children from a young age. Make space in your schedule after you read aloud to allow for oral narration; don't rush the process.
- Prepare for oral narration by listing difficult words, names, terms, and places on a board for the children to see to aid their narration. We're not tricking or testing; we're listening!
- Only read the text once; this encourages the habit of attention.

- If children are struggling to narrate, set an example and narrate from the text yourself, allowing them to hear what it sounds like.
- Write notes or make audio recordings of their narrations as a record of their progress.
- Try creating a book of centuries to help make learning stick. This is basically a visual timeline in a book (or binder). It's a really simple, fun way to record anyone and everyone you meet from history during your studies and conversations. Across each double-page spread label the century and time span of years (e.g., 16th century: AD 1501–1600) and go all the way back to 4000 BC (or whenever you want). Children can write, draw, or stick in a picture representing a person or story they've studied in that period of history.
- Consider using narration in different circumstances: ask children to retell stories from films, YouTube documentaries, audio podcasts, song lyrics, or even interviews with grandparents about their experiences.
- Coax a reluctant narrator by using an open-ended creative question such as "Describe the characters in the book as if you were describing a good friend" or "Tell me three things you've learnt from this story."
- After you have finished a story, build in time for children to go off and play out aspects of the people, places, and plotlines.
- Ask your child to try a new creative way to tell something back to you. Try LEGO reenactments. Use Play-Doh to make characters from stories. Comic book strips can retell a whole story (a popular one in our home). Make a video narrating to the camera. Record a radio show interview about the topic. Draw or paint a picture. The only limits are a child's imagination and your patience.

Chapter 6

Treasurers of Living Books

We want a wider range of knowledge than the life about us affords,
and books are our best teachers.

CHARLOTTE MASON, *OURSELVES*

Living *is the apt word Charlotte Mason used to describe the types*
of books that she encouraged children to read and engage with
as part of a holistic curriculum. Living books usually have one
passionate author; have an enthusiastic, narrative style; are
page-turners; and are easy to talk about afterwards.

Books That Mark the Chapters of Our Lives

I recently bought a monogram seal stamp to emboss the books our
family has collected or inherited over the years. It proudly marks each
text with a simple imprinted circle stating "Boden Library, Est. 2000."
My family often finds me quietly stamping away with delight, much
to their personal bemusement. I love the idea that no matter where my
books finally end up, either gracing my children's own home libraries
or scattered around the country, the new owner will know where they
came from and that they were treasured.

Books mark moments and memories in every chapter of childhood. You'd often find my father engrossed in theology and in history, whilst my mother loved (and still does) drama, mystery, and romance. Watching them read voraciously was a beautiful beginning and a glorious combination for me as a child wondering what to take off the shelf. Nowadays you'll generally find me alternating between my parents' favourite genres at the opposing ends of the bookshelf.

My father regularly sent us to the red, hardback collection of dictionaries on the bottom shelf of the brown wooden bookcase in our living room to look up and research an unfamiliar word. He'd never let us get away with laziness by quickly answering our question "Dad, what does this mean?" Nowadays, my children just ask Alexa! My mother read aloud to us and would gather our friends as part of the "Monday club" to read stories of adventure and faith. We'd listen intently to her warm voice, then endlessly discuss the events from the current chapter before completing what seemed like a trip to an imaginary world with delicious snacks and thirst-quenching drinks. As a child I loved devouring anything by Enid Blyton, losing myself in the antics at Malory Towers or uncovering village mysteries with the Famous Five. As I widened my variety of reading and grew more advanced in my academics, I developed a sound appetite for poetry, Shakespeare, and the Brontës which still lives in me today. Books are for loving as well as for learning.

I recognised quite early on the endorphin hit I experienced whilst wandering the aisles of a bookshop: no need to purchase, pursuing was enough. I learnt to crack open a vintage book and breathe in the story from the scent. There is no other smell quite like that of a well-loved library or bookshop! Happily, my youngest child has picked up this book sniffing trait, whilst the others still think it's rather strange. This thrill of a book, the drawing in of story, and the lingering "scent" of the emotional impact a tale can have upon us is exactly what Charlotte wanted children to get from their schoolbooks.

Charlotte saw no lasting value in the dry and stale facts often found in standard textbooks. She saw education as the stirring of emotion leading to a lasting imprint on the mind and soul. It made sense to her that learning could be built, brick by brick, upon ideas gathered from living books, experiences, observations, and hands-on encounters. As she states in one of her volumes of writing, "The way such teaching should come to us is, here a little and there a little, incidentally, from books which we read for the interest of the story, the beauty of the poem, or the grace of the writing."[1]

Charlotte taught us the term "living books" to help aid us in our choosing of materials for our children; these are books (and resources) that bring enjoyment, foster connections, and stir delight for the learner. A living book is a gift in the hand of the reader and an offering of thought straight from the writer. A child who reads for themselves or is read to from a living book is being offered the opportunity to connect with "other persons of all sorts and conditions, of all countries and climes, of all times, past and present."[2] We imagine the author peering over the shoulder of the reader, waiting to see what ideas they will pick up on and take for themselves. Each child is different, each connection worthy.

So how do we learn to discern which books qualify? We might start to sift through suggested lists online and make requests across social media, but it is far easier to make our own choices based on a set of simple questions. Aside from the basics such as "Is it written by one passionate author?" we have to ask ourselves, "Is it actually interesting?" To find this out quickly I often do the one-page test; next time you're at the library or a bookshop, take a book from the shelf, read one page, and ask yourself, "Does the beginning of this book beckon me to read on? Does it keep my attention and draw me in? Does it leave a lasting impression that confirms it will be a page-turner?" If you are bored of the book, your children will be too. Following on from that initial glance, we can test if it can be read aloud with ease, enabling a child to listen and talk about it comfortably. The longer we visit the shelves of living books, the easier it becomes to recognise them.

Books That Are Written with Passion

What we find common to the authors of living books is a deep sense of infectious passion about the subject. Charlotte often stressed that these texts have one dedicated writer, as opposed to a group of editors assembling facts alongside appealing photography. Biographies, novels, poems, dramas, and fairy tales all provide a wondrous variety of ideas to enhance a child's holistic learning experience.

A wonderful memory from the past few years of our homeschool journey is reading Marita Conlon-McKenna's trilogy which follows the pain and plight of the O'Driscoll family, starting with the book *Under the Hawthorn Tree*. This Irish family faced tragedy and suffering during the potato famine, losing loved ones as well as their sense of identity. As the books progress, we follow their quest to find distant relatives and travel with thirteen-year-old Peggy O'Driscoll as she faces a challenging journey across the Atlantic to America.

My children and I greatly anticipated each reading session, aching for the characters as their losses unfolded relentlessly across generations. We talked about the characters as if they were real people, and we grieved over the final few pages, with my youngest exclaiming, "I don't want it to end." This trilogy gave us insight into some real history and geography, but even greater than that, my children learnt incomparable examples of compassion, strength, dignity, and resilience. Inevitably these fictional characters will help my children find their own character in real life.

There isn't a theme, topic, or form of instruction for life that we can't find in literature. Books contain hidden wonder ready for the observant reader to uncover and add to their experience of life. Living ideas and words don't just stay on a page after being heard; they are digested, discussed, and presented time and time again through conversations, narrations, and creativity, and they play a part in an intentional, fascinating life.

Living books have the power to not only invite the reader into the heart of the story but to connect the reader to the mind of the author. Charlotte wanted children to connect with great thinkers who were passionate about science, nature, history, geography, and even architecture. The greatest of historical minds have written the greatest of books; we don't get to hear interviews on podcasts, see television interviews, or read about them in the paper, but we do get insight into their minds and souls by reading their words. Poets, novelists, and playwrights naturally lead us on a journey of heart and mind that follows the path they travelled themselves.

Books That Make It on Your List

There is a common thought that Charlotte Mason's actual book recommendations are now archaic and not relevant for twenty-first-century education. The Parents' National Education Union (PNEU) was an organisation providing resources and support for teachers and home-schoolers in the United Kingdom in the early twentieth century in accordance with the educational ideas of Charlotte Mason. Many see the PNEU listings or suggested timetables and can't for one minute imagine their skateboard-loving, digital-content-creating child ever reading, let alone enjoying, the texts. The teachings and style of long bygone authors, poets, and playwrights can appear distant and irrelevant to the world our children are growing up in. Ironically, even in Charlotte's day her critics commented on the seemingly archaic choice of texts, but she insisted "The fact that they have not been allowed to die proves in itself that the authors have that to say, and a way of saying it, which the world cannot do without."[3]

There are many dedicated readers who devour classic literature because it contains timeless intriguing stories, historical insights, and unarguably excellent writing. The living ideas from these stories impact our character and conduct. But the list of books we curate for our family does not have to be limited to some sort of preapproved catalogue from the past. We do not have to tick off every text from a popular homeschool forum for fear of being visited by the homeschool police!

As we list our books to read, we must also try to find variety in genre and style as much as we want to explore a plethora of topics. Novels and drama bring us vibrant examples of character growth and teach us how to overcome difficulty. Poetry can provide "a thousand thoughts that burn" that come to us "on the wings of verse."[4] This genre not only critiques life but also inspires us to keep living well. Charlotte stated that "most of us carry in our minds tags of verse which shape our conduct more than we know."[5] Fairy tales serve up moral notions, whilst history and biography warn us through tragic examples and inspire us through noble ones. The list could go on; but this we know, when chosen well, the feast of literature feeds the mind and sustains the soul through childhood and beyond. Through my research (and from personal experience) I have found that for a child to really engage with a person, a place, or a passion; a subject, a part of the world, or a scientific concept, there must be an element of personal discovery and owning of a concept. Charlotte describes this as if a child is digging for knowledge and forming a place in their mind (and soul) where it can sit forever.[6] I always try to look for books that allow us to slow down and deepen the learning experience both for enjoyment and longevity.

Charlotte advises us to learn to discern what a living book is through reading, connecting, and continuing to curate our own lists and libraries.[7] Over the years I've sometimes become so accustomed to looking at recommendation lists, seeing images of books used by other families on social media, or just reading with my younger children what worked with my older children, that I've stopped looking and learning for myself.

I was recently in Oxford for the day with my family, and whereas I usually frequent the used bookshops, I decided to step inside a huge well-known British bookstore for a change. Everything smelled new and fresh, and there were mid-aisle risers filled with appealing book-themed gifts and trinkets. I saw the sign for the history section and stayed there for a while. Whilst picking up a few titles, I did my usual one-page test to see if they fit my living book criteria. Most of them did. There were rows upon rows of recently published living history books that landed on a new list for me. I came home with one on the kings and queens of England that I never would have found otherwise, and we began to read immediately. I learnt that day that even with the enormity of the booklists and recommendations within Charlotte Mason circles, if I was to truly find my freedom, then I must stay alert and continue to acquaint myself with authors slightly younger than Lamb, Nesbit, and Plutarch!

It's easy to become blinkered in our book choices; as much as I have loved and valued the reading inspiration of wise and learned educators, I am itching to see twenty-first-century families bravely learning from current authors, sharing their new finds, and maybe, just maybe beginning to write living books themselves. Let's keep our eyes open and our browsers closed a little more. Why not step inside your local independent bookshop or even your large city store and see what's waiting for you and your modern-reading family?

Books That Help People See Themselves

If books really do open a wide window to the world, then it is important that we learn to read wide, deep, and high. The trouble with nineteenth- or twentieth-century literature is that it cannot be removed from its original time. For all their literary brilliance, truthful insight about the human condition, or historic teaching, some of these old stories can also bring with them gender stereotypes, blatant racism, body shaming, and many other kinds of discrimination. Children across the world often find themselves misrepresented or omitted altogether in the stories they read.

I have recognised how easy it is to become desensitised to these ideas through literature and therefore at risk of passing them on to my children. For example, we might do this by ignoring discrimination in a story or by skipping past racist language or behaviour. We quickly justify discriminatory stereotypes by commenting how the author "didn't know any better" or "they're just a product of their time." But unless we find a better way to navigate the past, we can end up stuck in history. We don't have to be afraid to put a book down if needed, but we can also be bold enough to face the truth of that time. My suggestion isn't to do away with every book written before the twenty-first century; but there may indeed be some you will want to rightfully leave alone. It is vital that we grow in discernment when opening literature to our children and that we deal directly with the mistreatment or misrepresentation of any character, human or animal.

In the late 1980s, Emily Style, writing for the National SEED Project, introduced the world of education to the concept of "curriculum as window and mirror."[8] Using this idea, author and speaker Amber O'Neal Johnston has spoken powerfully regarding the lack of diversity in our lists of living books. She writes about how books can be used to help children learn to love themselves and others; she also describes our need to provide "mirrors and windows" for all our children. Books can be like mirrors that reflect who the child is, and books can be like windows that give an insight into other cultures and ways of life. This understanding helps us frame our choices and line our shelves. Amber recently helped bring the poems of Harlem Renaissance writer Effie Lee Newsome back into publication (with Living Book

Press). I love how in the newly printed foreword for the poems she describes the collection as being for every child, "reflecting the everyday life recognized as their own or a window giving a rare view into the playful romps and observations of brown-skinned children."[9]

The UK charity BookTrust also refers to the notion of "mirrors and windows" in their 2019 research to address diversity within British children's literacy. Despite the children's book sector thriving, the group discovered that "the cohort of people that creates these books does not reflect the makeup of the UK, where an array of lives, cultures, identities and stories have overlapped for many years." The research goes on to reveal and challenge how

> the absence of an inclusive range of characters, or creative
> role models, in children's literature has the potential to deter
> children from minority backgrounds from reading and
> experiencing the associated benefits. In turn, this lack of
> engagement with reading could deter children from pursuing
> careers in writing and/or drawing and further embed the
> imbalance.[10]

This makes me want to ensure that we help our children read stories of heroes who represent all nations, colours, tribes, and tongues. Let's read and reveal real history together. May we not limit Black history (or the history of any other marginalized group) to one month but weave it into the rhythms of our year.

You may not realise until you start really looking just how lacking in diversity your reading selections have been. Baroness Floella Benjamin first began her journey into the British public eye through children's television. She recalls in an interview how, in the mid-1970s, she challenged her producer on the choices of literature being read and the illustrations being shown on the television programmes for young children. Floella recalls the conversation by saying, "I'm telling the story . . . and sometimes I'm saying it in my Caribbean accent, but all the imagery on the screen, all the illustrations are white; can't we have some Black and Asian and Chinese faces?" After which the producer naively answered, "Oh, we hadn't noticed." Floella says that from that day on, the Children's BBC became the most diverse corner of British television.[11] Baroness Benjamin has gone on to write many books for children, telling stories that depict her experiences as a young Caribbean woman. She is a renowned advocate for all children, stating that "childhood lasts a lifetime, so the earlier young children are conscious of the emotions they go through when you are different, no matter what that might be, the better it is to be all embracing and have empathy for differences. Tolerance, compassion and consideration are the key to happiness."[12] Change happens only when we choose to notice.

Children with disabilities or rare conditions also often find themselves ignored or misrepresented in literature. In 2015 British mother and author Kristina Gray wrote the children's story *Strong and Mighty Max*. The lead character in the story, Max, is based on her son Samuel, who was born with a rare condition, achondroplasia, the most common form of dwarfism. Kristina quickly learnt that one of the biggest challenges Samuel would face in life would be navigating other people's perceptions of him based on presentations of dwarfism in the media and culture. As a result of this she decided to write a children's story that would help to educate his peers about his condition and provide a positive role model for children born with rare conditions. Kristina's bravery and skill represent the heart of every mother feeling the pain of their child. We may not all write books to raise awareness of the difficulties our children may face, but we can all make a start by considering the stories we read and opening the eyes and hearts of the bold thinkers we raise.

Living books, old and new, can play a part in helping us gain a deeper understanding of the life experiences of those who are different from ourselves. They draw us into the pain of others and stir our empathy so we desire to make things better for the next generation. In all of these stories in this chapter, individuals have felt the pain and desired to make it better for their children and the next generation. As curators of lists of books for our own families, we must take the time to search far and wide for books that tell all kinds of stories about all kinds of people.

Books That Form Connections

Amid a difficult 2020 spent largely in lockdown with my children due to the global pandemic, we were regularly hearing speeches from worldwide political leaders as well as listening to press conferences held by UK prime minister Boris Johnson and his cabinet. Many different styles of leadership were demonstrated, highlighted, and scrutinised left, right, and centre by the media and the masses. During this period of volatile global shifts, our family sought to keep a consistent rhythm of learning, even as the rest of the world had a temporary taste of trying to school at home. As part of our planned reading, we explored the work of Plutarch on the life of Julius Caesar. We also delved deeply into the story of Daniel from the Old Testament in the Bible. As my children read and told back their interpretation of the stories, they drew connections between the ancient and modern leaders. Our conversations compared strategy, the treatment of others, the impact of ego, and what kind of a leader makes a positive or negative impact. I was amazed at how poignant and unplanned the timing of this all was. Ancient texts had collided with modern contexts.

What I experienced during that time was a glimpse of light in a dark season. I saw how important it was to develop leadership values in my own children, not only from experience and through example, but from the good, bad, and ugly stories of others both on the literary page and on the literal world stage. This would have been no surprise to Charlotte, who knew the power in living books to help children make living connections with the wider world. She highlighted that books are our best teachers because they allow us to be *one step removed* and make judgements on the values and decisions of others. By reading and engaging with living books, our children can gain a fresh sense of morality, and stories can shape their conduct whilst giving them guidance for life. In looking through the lens of others, we can begin to shape perspectives for ourselves as "what is properly called literature, that is, poetry, essays, the drama, and novels, is perhaps the most useful for our moral instruction, because the authors bring their insight to bear in a way they would hesitate to employ when writing about actual persons."[13] Reading isn't just for developing academic competence but truly plays a part in developing our children's moral guidance, emotional development, and sense of self.

Books That Avoid the Trouble of *Twaddle*

Those who are more familiar with the writings of Charlotte Mason will recognise her disdain of unhelpful books for children and her quaint use of the word "twaddle."[14] Our interpretations and strength of conviction around what constitutes "twaddle" can differ, but it generally is a description of dry and boring textbooks that give facts, spoon-feed information to children, and have an array of authors and contributors, thus watering down the "voice." Unfortunately, this word has and can be bandied around in a rather pretentious and judgemental manner and can create barriers for the child's sense of agency within their growing relationship with books.

Whilst we will likely preselect and present an array of "the best" living books for our children's academic development, current research also shows that if we hope for children to have an ongoing love for reading, there must be an element of choice for themselves. The UK charity BookTrust has discovered through their research that choice must be at the centre of a reading life.[15] When my children were younger, I'd leave baskets of books around the house—at the bottom of their bed, next to the fireplace, on the shelf near the dining table. They were free to take, flick, and enjoy at their pleasure. If our home libraries are full of interesting titles, fascinating settings, and intriguing characters, then we don't have to worry too much about making every decision for them. We simply drown out the "twaddle" with the terrific and let them choose!

Don't just eliminate—educate. Most respected nutritionists will now advise that quickly eliminating certain unhealthy foods altogether can cause a mental struggle with willpower that feeds a sense of deprivation. Instead, they recommend introducing and adding in more fruit, vegetables, and whole grain, leaving little room for those other foods. Introduction is more powerful than elimination. We all enjoy a drive-through burger now and again, but there's nothing quite as satiating as a slowly prepared and cooked home meal full of colour, texture, and flavour. I'd say the same for books! Carefully curate your bookshelves by regularly visiting the local library where possible, and take your children to your favourite secondhand bookshop to browse, touch the books, and inhale that glorious smell!

Our youngest son is an enthusiastic illustrator; he's already planning a future career working with film, games, or books, and it's important to him that he sees this in action now and finds examples of creators doing this kind of work. Whilst our days are filled with poetry, literature, history, and nature, his spare time and bedroom shelves are brimming with colourful cartoon and graphic stories, film inspiration, and Marvel movies! His comic books may not mean much to me, but they are special to him and therefore worth treasuring. Maybe what constitutes twaddle is sometimes in the eye of the beholder.

Books That Awaken the Soul

It was Charlotte's mission to reach all parents and children with her educational ideas, but due to national learning requirements and inspections, her somewhat radical teachings and methods initially only really reached the middle classes or those who were able to connect with the PNEU. However, just under a decade before she died, a wonderful expansion of her work caught her attention. As her team of kindred spirits grew, some took up Charlotte's mantle to seek educational breakthroughs in less fortunate parts of the country such as the mining villages. Charlotte writes about this in the preface of *Towards a Philosophy of Education*, delighting that "the 'soul' of a class of children in a mining village school awoke simultaneously at this magic touch and has remained awake." She also records that "the ardour for knowledge in the children of this mining village is a phenomenon that indicates new possibilities."[16]

This class of students in an impoverished town was given a selection of living books and an opportunity to tell back their ideas, and a whole new world opened to them. Such was the impact on the school that they even converted the inspectors who were wowed by their vocabulary, imagination, and expression! Living books were found to have a compound effect on so many other aspects of the children's formal education. This news brought much hope and expectation to Charlotte in her later years, leading her to coin the phrase that opens this book: "It may be that the souls of all children are waiting for the call of knowledge to awaken them to delightful living."[17]

The obvious transformation in this small cottage school—as well as many others across the UK—was triggered by the gift of a small collection of living books; books that told a story, held truth, and connected the reader to great minds. The educators who shared these books did so with a strong belief that if teachers would trust the mind of the child, these stories and tales would do their work. And if living books really can change the life of children from a poor Victorian mining village, then I am certain they can do the same for your children too.

TAKE A MASON MOMENT:
Suggestions for Learning from Living Books

- Do the one-page test: next time you're at the library or a bookshop, take a book from the shelf, read one page, and ask yourself, Does the beginning of this book beckon me to read on?
- Remember, living books don't have to be old—modern authors are writing living literature all the time; keep your eyes open and make room on your library shelves.
- Shop your own shelves. Before you go out and buy something new, remind yourself about what you already have in your collection!
- Raid library sales and secondhand shops—over the years I've rarely paid full price for a book; it doesn't have to be an expensive process!
- Create a little shelf of living books that you can "grab and go" at any time.
- Include your children in the process; don't do it all for them. Have fun deciding what a living book is to your family.
- Use mealtimes (or even just breakfast) to gather children and to help them sit still for at least ten minutes. Keep your readings short, varied, and interesting whilst your children are munching their cereal and sipping their juice.
- Use audiobooks if you're out and about in the car, but remember to pause after each chapter so your children can process what they've heard.
- Create cozy, memorable moments around books (especially if you're getting that groaning noise when you announce, "Hey

kids, let's read together."). Grab blankets, tea, and a snack, snuggle up together, and get to work on those wonderful words.

- Have books around: line your shelves, fill baskets, and pop small tubs of them in children's bedrooms. Just having books in view is proven to engage children's interest and creates an appetite and curiosity to explore what's inside them.
- Make sure your children see you with a book in hand (or listening to an audiobook whilst you fold laundry) and talk to them about what you're reading.
- When choosing a living book, there are several key questions you and your children can answer together to determine if it is worth finishing.

> » Do you love/like the book?
> » Is it interesting?
> » Does it fuel the mind and soul?
> » Can your child find themselves represented in the story?
> » Does the story offer an opportunity to see into a culture or context different from your own?
> » Does it keep your attention and draw you in? Can you/your children narrate from it easily?
> » Can you read it aloud with ease? Can a child listen to it comfortably?
> » Is it written by one passionate author?
> » Does it leave a mark/lasting impression, or is it forgettable?
> » Is it a page-turner? Are you expectant to find out more about the characters and plot?

Chapter 7

Explorers of Nature Study

We were all meant to be naturalists, each in his degree,
and it is inexcusable to live in a world so full of the marvels
of plant and animal life and to care for none of these things.
CHARLOTTE MASON, *HOME EDUCATION*

Charlotte Mason believed that when our children see, engage with,
and take note of nature, it is a holistic experience; their minds, bodies,
and souls entwine with the beauty around them, and that beauty
begins to take up space in their hearts alongside the other memories
and experiences they have gathered. Studying nature is an entry point
into the practice of paying attention with our senses, a foundation for
other subjects, and a wonderful way to experience the world.

Finding Charlotte in the Meadows

Whilst many modern home educators have seen Charlotte's name
hashtagged via Instagram homeschooling circles, discovered a blog
where she is mentioned, or even read the well-known book *For the
Children's Sake* by Susan Schaeffer Macaulay, most people tend to come
to Charlotte Mason on the wings of nature. Lynn Seddon, a well-
known UK Charlotte Mason authority and the author of *Exploring
Nature with Children*, was a fellow English home educator as I was

first starting out over fifteen years ago. Our eldest children were of a similar age, and we struck up a lasting friendship via the joys of the internet. Lynn was slightly ahead of the game, and her website Raising Little Shoots featured a blog I frequented during our two years of avid research in the lead-up to deciding whether we should homeschool our children or not. Once we'd started, I emailed Lynn asking, "Where did you start with the Charlotte Mason philosophy?" to which she answered (but doesn't even remember), "Start with nature study."

I was raised in Yorkshire, England, which is known for its rolling hills, glorious coastlines, and of course, Emily Brontë's *Wuthering Heights*. Wild beauty can be seen on every horizon, and my childhood was immersed in undulating green landscapes dotted with the shape of sheep. The village we lived in overlooked farmers' fields that changed colour in every season; we could see Bradford to the right and, on a clear day, Halifax to the left. The sun came up at the front of our house, and most evenings we witnessed dramatic sunsets bringing the day to a close. At the bottom end of our street was the entrance to an ancient woodland site called Stoneycliffe Woods. The woods are famous for bluebells and wild garlic in spring, breeding birds in summer, and fungi in autumn. Before the 1998 amendment to the Wildlife and Countryside Act banned locals from picking bluebells, we used to gather them by the fistfuls and bring them home to place in glass jars around the house. My mother captured the essence of Stoneycliffe Woods in a poem titled "The Bluebell Wood" that she scribed after living in the village for just under a year.

> *The rustle of trees, the blue haze around*
> > *Hearing the cuckoo, what a beautiful sound.*
> *Bluebells are gathered, by children with glee.*
> > *Plenty are left for you and for me.*
>
> PATRICIA SHEFFIELD

Charlotte thought that children would do well to be immersed in nature as much as possible from the youngest of ages. She encouraged families living in all different parts of England, even in smoggy central London, to catch a bus to the countryside and allow their children to explore. I was blessed in that I didn't need to get on a bus to discover what she was talking about. The quintessential English sound of the cuckoo awakened spring mornings in our small village, and the familiar *hoohoo* of the owl brought comfort to dusk. My mother took us on nature walks where we liked to gather and forage anything colourful, shiny, or unusual. We didn't necessarily know the names of species, draw them, or even talk about them; but we did observe them. We valued time outdoors and didn't have to be forced or cajoled into it. We knew the familiar sights from walking in the woods and nature reserves through each season. Nature is ingrained deep in my soul, as a byproduct of the beauty we lived amongst.

Children know the joy of the land more than anyone I know; they know the freedom of running in a field, spinning round and round, climbing trees, and jumping in puddles, and they are not afraid to get dirty. The beautiful innocence of a child outdoors is a wonder to experience, because everything is a wonder to them. The colours, smells, sounds, and sights of hours outdoors are magical to young children, and according to Charlotte, should form the foundation of their early education.

Nature as the Nurturer of Our Curriculum

Nature study can be a foundation to so many other subjects as we build our unique curriculum. When we step outdoors, we find the seeds of science, biology, physics, history, mathematics, and more. Our children may complain about the rain, snow, or hail, but we'd be smart to jump right in to teach a moment on geography by sharing the water cycle with them! A basic knowledge of direction and boundaries can be gleaned from navigating the garden or local park. I spent many moments in my early homeschooling days chalking "north, south, east, and west" on the paving of our backyard and showing my children the wonders of a moving needle on a compass. Nature study builds foundational skills such as observation, recording, and reporting back—tools for young scientists to use again and again in their investigations.

Being outdoors can inspire further reading about natural history, can give journal prompts for emerging writers, and may lead to a longing for nature-themed living stories, fables, and poetry. Nature study is not an extracurricular exercise but is fundamental to shaping the scientific skills children need to enhance study, observation, attention, and recall.

A child's burgeoning interest in nature represents a whole world of thought and opportunity. The smallest brooks lead to rivers, and then oceans; acorns become oak trees; and we all live under one big sky, sun, and moon. How wonderful for our children to grasp the great expanse of the world and the impact of each part of it on the others. I remember one of my children finally understanding time differences around the world and how the Earth moved around the sun: "Oh, so when it's breakfast time in Australia, I'm going to bed." I love those lights-on revelations that are so often triggered by engagement in the world of outdoors.

Those who have delved into volume 1 of Charlotte's series on education discover, often to their disbelief, that she recommends children under nine years old spend four to six hours outdoors every day.[1] Some young home educators take this advice explicitly to heart and stress to no end about the calculation of their hours outdoors. I've seen question after question from mothers on forums over the years asking how you possibly spend that amount of time outdoors without abandoning the home, laundry, cooking, or older children studying for exams. It should come as no surprise that I think this may be missing the point. The core advice is to spend as much time outside as possible, and this must work for your current climate, the area you live in, and the makeup of your family. The principle to weave into your daily rhythm is "Just get outside."

Making the Most of Where You Live

Nature offers the opportunity for children to experience the world around them and connect with it via their own senses. And the location you live in can help shape what this looks like, no matter your individual circumstances. I love seeing the incredible images online of the environments of some homeschoolers across the world. It is amazing to see the wonder of families who have made their homes in a wilderness, with picture-perfect cabins in the woods, or another free-range child frolicking amongst free-range chickens—yet the early years of our family's home educating life were not spent like this. We lived in a small, terraced house in an urban area, with three bedrooms, one bathroom, a small galley kitchen, and a backyard with no grass. Our space was small and our resources smaller, but we made the most of what we had. The grey slabs around the yard were edged with narrow flower beds, and each year we planted small trees, flowers, and shrubs, and we even attempted vegetables. One of my life mottoes is "Love where you live," and that was my full intention in this house we felt so blessed to call our own.

My four children grew in height and curiosity from the smallness and simplicity of our tiny backyard; we added a bird feeder, a wooden cabin, and a firepit, and we had everything we ever needed. I have lasting memories of Joel figuring out chords on the guitar around a late-summer roaring fire, Nyah reading on a blanket in the sunshine, Micah learning the compass points from my chalk markings on the ground, and Sienna, as a young, not-yet-verbal toddler, signing "bird" by repeatedly pushing her forefinger and thumb together after she'd observed a pied wagtail from the window before anyone else. These were our humble but glorious beginnings of utilising creation as a learning tool.

Though our house was in an urban area, just a few streets away was a simple green space called Moat House Park, which became our Eden. It was close enough for tired toddler legs and a mama pushing a stroller whilst carrying the youngest in a baby carrier. We learnt to experience this green space through every season; we observed the changing leaves in autumn, the bare twigs in winter, the bird song in spring, and the smells and sights of summer that had us picnicking for hours. To so many who lived in the area it was just somewhere to walk dogs and blow off the cobwebs on a cold Sunday afternoon. Yet to us, this was a haven of learning, a place to collect beauty and bugs, a space to never get bored of or complain about; it was an extension of our hearts and home. If this was all we ever had access to, I was convinced I could open my children's eyes and senses to the wonder and beauty of creation—whetting their appetites to sincerely seek out knowledge and understanding from the world themselves. The key to nature study is not the location of where we live, but how much we live in the location we find ourselves in.

Turning our eye to nature draws us to an ancient human privilege; a daily gift we take for granted because it's always there and always around us. No matter where we live, what our financial situation is, or what resources we have at our fingertips, we all live under the same sky, and the sun never fails to rise or set. The birds sing at just the right time, the buds always burst, and the flowers will bloom, whether we're looking at them or not. But why not look, why not pay attention, and why not teach our children to do the same? Let's not miss the daily opportunities to look up, to pause for a moment to listen, and to literally stop and smell the roses.

Nurturing the Habits of Nature

Our turning towards nature helps us focus our heart to seek things greater than ourselves. It is about learning to be at peace with those things we can't control. Years of research have revealed how vital being out in nature is to our mental health: from listening to water trickle, smelling the forest air, or staring at fractals and cobwebs, it all counts as a healing, soul-stirring endeavour that we'd do well to invest time in as much as we can. All children benefit from being outside whether homeschooled or otherwise. Sue Palma is a recently retired education officer from the New Forest National Park Authority in Hampshire, England. She speaks in a recent article entitled "Let Nature Be Your Teacher" (a reference to the Wordsworth poem "The Tables Turned") of the way that children in all forms of education seem to naturally grow in confidence and come alive outdoors.

> We've welcomed underprivileged kids, many with real problems in their school or home life, but among the trees, even those who can be uncooperative in the classroom become calm. I'll always remember one boy with behavioural difficulties being as good as gold and declaring his time in the Forest as "The best day of my life." I've seen elective mutes start to talk, because in the Forest there's no such thing as a stupid question. And when we've asked questions, those "failing" at school are often the first to answer.[2]

I love the thought that it is harder to fail in the forest. Rich work takes place when we intentionally set up our days around observing nature to build both our confidence and our skill set. So often we start by asking how we implement a particular methodology; we look for resources and inspiration in order for us to "do it right." But there is no right way to use our senses; we just need to lead the way and inspire our children to lean into the sights and sounds around them and allow them to take up room in their minds and hearts. There's no formula to falling in love with flora and fauna, but when children see and experience the world with all their senses, their curiosity will grow. Loving nature is the gateway to learning about nature.

We can teach our children about the blackbird being a fabulous songbird, or we can sit outside on a spring morning and listen to the melodic sounds of a real blackbird perched high on a rooftop. Nature needs to be seen, felt, and smelt. Books only build upon the foundation of grass between toes, leaves in hair, and a real live newt in your hand. Nature is the space where the seeds of understanding are planted deep.

Connecting Nature with Journaling

Charlotte encouraged children to sketch or brush draw a selection of their natural observations in a notebook, asking students to make lists of first appearances of nature throughout the year and, more than anything, to keep looking. Over the years I've watched many a homeschooling mother pull her hair out trying to "get it right" when it comes to nature journaling, whilst provoking tears from her children who also aren't enjoying the process. Nature journaling is a creative form of remembering and recording and requires time and practice to develop skill, but I am not sure we need to be so concerned about getting it right.

In Charlotte's time, children would have used basic paint, ink, and paper, yet nowadays we have digital photography and drawing software, online photograph journals, countless forms of drawing and painting equipment, and apps to help us record our observations within the natural world. Skill can be learnt and taught over time, but don't sweat the sketch, or your frustrated children will make tearful associations with the recording of nature. Spend more time looking at the object than looking at the paper, and the rest will come with practice. In our home, we use photography, graphite paper, tracing paper, pencils, and paint to record our seasonal observations from the world around us. We keep it simple but consistent, and we continue to care. That's the goal.

Young children can begin to identify and record in their notebooks petal counts, the length of stem, the colour of the pollen, and the time of year each flower appears. Learning to observe and jot down thoughts and pictures of what they've seen can cultivate care and expand their knowledge of everything from animal tracks, phases of the moon, through to the changing of trees in the autumn.

Connecting Nature with Literature

Charlotte discouraged using books as the primary means of understanding the natural world for young children; she placed a constant emphasis on them being outdoors and being left alone. But she did say that all this "common information" and their early observations would form "a capital groundwork for a scientific education."[3] Books are not the primary learning tool in our study of nature, but they do corroborate and provide further inspiration for our children's observations.

For example, a book may give insight into the nesting behaviour of a thrush your child has just heard (but may not have seen up close), or a poem may gently describe the mountain view your child has admired many times. Poetry such as Robert Louis Stevenson's "The Cow" or Christina Rossetti's "The Caterpillar" can help a child understand how a writer sees those animals. Our children will no doubt come alive hearing the stories of Peter Rabbit and the other countryside tales of Beatrix Potter or get lost in Francis Hodgson Burnett's *The Secret Garden* along with dreams of finding a key to their own adventure.

My younger children and I recently spent a whole year with Wordsworth; although I diligently took time to present a wide view of his varied poetry, what my children remember most is Wordsworth as a "nature poet." When the celandines dotted the local riverside and field that spring, our minds went to his poetry again. There's something quite comforting about reciting Wordsworth's observations from the early 1800s when they continue to repeat themselves in the twenty-first century.

> *There is a flower, the lesser celandine,*
> *That shrinks, like many more, from cold and rain;*
> *And, the first moment that the sun may shine,*
> *Bright as the sun himself, 'tis out again!*[4]

I remember once watching a live online performance written in collaboration with poet Robert Macfarlane and artist Jackie Morris, who desired to bring lost words from nature back into the lives of children. Their powerful orchestral rendition was both haunting and moving, featuring songs about a goldfinch, a willow tree, and an acorn. Each piece of music echoed the simplicity and innocence that nature represents in a child's life. After I played the goldfinch track to my children one morning, we read beautiful stories about this bird, learning how they place flower petals in their nests and eat in high places. We've since admired goldfinch art, painted them in our nature journals, and recognised their high-pitched song amongst the trees. But I will never forget the day in our small urban terraced house (where only starlings and sparrows occasionally paid us a visit) when we saw real live goldfinches appear on the front lawn to enjoy the spiky seed heads of something that had grown there! All four of my children were at the window in wide-eyed amazement wondering what we had done to deserve such a royal visit from these "little gifts of light."[5] Though they never came back, the wondrous memory of their visit always did. Perhaps it is in this space where art, poetry, music, and nature come together that deep connections can be made.

Connecting Nature with Life

A few years ago, I was honoured to share the stage at a conference in California with John Muir Laws, avid nature observer, artist, and author of books which help us engage with the world around us. Jack (as he's known) didn't just wax eloquent from the stage; he took the eager delegates on a nature walk to show us how he engages with the world and how he journals for the joy of the heart. I learnt that day that Jack always fills out three statements about what he finds. These statements are equally wonderful for children to engage with as they're exploring the world around them:

I notice . . .
I wonder . . .
It reminds me of . . .

I love how these statements take us away from the idea that we should just look for something in nature and report on it in a notebook to be "marked" by a teacher later. The statements help the observer engage with what they've seen, and they shift the emphasis away from formulaic instruction and—dare I say—curriculum, leading our children to an open road of discovery.

Children are wonderfully inquisitive; they are experts at asking "why," and as they become observers of nature, they move towards natural investigation of whatever catches their eye. We'd do well to leave their minds to investigate as the ant disappears through the crack in the kitchen wall, or as the bunny speedily hops across the country road and they wonder where it has gone. Leave them intrigued as the poppy head turns red and the seeds shake within the pod. Let them figure out how the horse chestnut hits the ground in autumn, opening to reveal a shiny brown conker. As we watch how they lean in and learn, we realise how much we still have to learn ourselves. There is no substitute for this kind of real-world observation.

I confess that it is a little frustrating for me to see how much nature study can sometimes slide into the world of prepackaged overcommercialisation. It is easy to purchase a curriculum where all the work is done for us. We can buy printables, study bundles, and subscription boxes, and we can learn about different regional variations of birds and beasts. We can send our children to forest school for a week or to a nature club for a day and then tick a box to tell ourselves it's done. All these things can play a part in our home education experience, but they shouldn't be the whole picture. To truly turn our children's hearts and thinking towards the beauty of the world around them, they must be in it on a regular basis. It is not about colouring in nature, but about letting nature add colour to our lives. Never let a lack of ink in your printer become a barrier to the power of really being present with nature. Allowing nature to be a very normal part of a child's learning days cultivates a reverence for life. Oh, to pull on boots, zip up a coat, and just walk! To be quiet, to sit on a log, to listen, and absorb all that is growing and living around us.

Charlotte encouraged a nature walk, not a nature talk; this can be hard with happy, chatty children, but on every walk, whether with a group or just my children, I encourage a moment of quiet to listen, look, and breathe in our surroundings. The more you walk, slowly absorbing the beauty of nature, the more your children will begin to see. As a child observes a tree season by season, closely watches a spider wrap its prey in silk, or sees the sun rise and set throughout the year, they collect a catalogue of understanding. Without even opening a book or watching a David Attenborough documentary, they observe for themselves and gain understanding of the natural world. Nature study cultivates wonder in a child; from the turning leaves in autumn to the miraculous metamorphosis of a caterpillar to a butterfly, there is so much to be in awe of in nature.

Most people know that early May is the best time in the northern hemisphere to hear the dawn chorus, but what you may not know is that the first Sunday of May is known as International Dawn Chorus Day. Last year a few friends and I started something that I hope will become an annual tradition. We gathered a group of nature-loving mothers at 4:30 a.m. at the beginning of May to capture our feathered friends' morning call. We gathered with fresh coffee and parabolic microphones (a form of homemade listening device) and headed to the woods just as the first few birds began their song. We whispered as if we were walking the creaky floorboards of an old-beloved library and breathed deeply the smell of wild garlic and bluebells. Hearing creation's concert is a bonding exercise that takes mothers out of the ordinary. As we walked the woods, watched the sun rise, and lived fully in the light of nature, we embodied for a moment all that we desired to pass on to our children.

TAKE A MASON MOMENT:
Suggestions for Nurturing Nature Study

- Start small—take a daily stroll around the garden or a local green area, and observe what stands out in that season.
- Keep a basket of smooth shells, pine cones, sea glass, or other natural treasures for young children to hold and become familiar with. I still have a box of these on hand for when young children come to visit.
- Learn about what's local and in your child's eyesight: a tree that can be seen from your kitchen window, garden birds, local wildflowers, and the sky from your apartment window. Become an expert on that bird, tree, or species!

- Bring nature treasures indoors and research ways of preserving, storing, and observing beauty, even when you can't get outside.
- Find friends to walk with—children are more likely to walk further and learn from each other's nature interests amid community.
- Don't sweat the sketch! Tracing paper or carbon paper can be a great tool for journaling beginners. Work from field guides or printed pictures of things you've seen outside and record them in your own journal—with whatever medium you choose.
- Buy a bargain page-per-week diary and add into your morning rhythm a habit of writing down the temperature and a doorstep observation. Note the changes over the weeks—you could even plot a temperature graph.
- Take photos, use identification apps, or journal on Instagram—it's all a form of reflecting and remembering. There's no such thing as "cheating"; all these tools aid our connection with the natural world.
- Get up early and listen to the Dawn Chorus.
- Read diaries, stories, and poems about nature to spark interest and cultivate care for the sustainability of our world.
- Get yourself on a boat in water.
- Watch nature documentaries to follow famous naturalists and videographers into places you and your children may never reach but still care about and are interested in.
- Stop what you are doing and go outside!

Chapter 8

Investors in Cultural Capital

There are few joys in life greater and more constant than our joy in Beauty.
CHARLOTTE MASON, *OURSELVES*

*Whether through picture or composer study, poetry, or music,
it is the aspects of culture that are woven throughout our lives
that make a rich Charlotte Mason education. She transformed
the previously high culture elements of a privileged lifestyle
into everyday offerings, for every child.*

Culture as a Catalyst for Learning

It was the French anthropologist Pierre Bourdieu who first introduced the notion that the amount of social, cultural, and economic capital we have determines our position in the world. His idea of "cultural capital" is broken down into three parts, namely, embodied cultural capital (how we speak and hold ourselves in society); objectified cultural capital (our tangible possessions or experiences through books, art, and music); and institutionalised cultural capital (our qualifications and training). The combination a person had of these three determined one's cultural class. So those in the higher echelons of society spoke and acted in eloquent ways, were exposed to the richness of the arts, and had the right qualifications for success. On the other hand, those in low society did not quite make the mark or have the same opportunities. The challenge with this kind of thinking is that so often cultural exposure is predetermined by family background, hierarchy, status, and wealth. Even before Bourdieu, Charlotte Mason set out to smash the idea that enriching culture was exclusive to the rich and privileged.

Cultural literacy is an offshoot of the idea of cultural capital coined by American educator E. D. Hirsch, and it refers to a person's ability to thrive and participate in any given culture. Just as a literate reader must know the components of the alphabet, grammar, and vocabulary to be fluent in a language, so too a culturally literate person must learn to engage with a culture's own stories, signs, symbols, and systems to thrive. In his book *Cultural Literacy*, Hirsch argues that "to be culturally literate is to possess the basic information needed to thrive in the modern world."[1] In other words, exposing our children to good culture is key to teaching them the invisible metrics of how to succeed holistically in life.

Despite some experts' disagreement about the benefit of cultural capital, the UK educational system has taken on the call to enrich children's lives with their own modern version of objectified cultural capital. As well as requiring a high standard of academic attainment, the board overseeing English schools (the Office for Standards in Education, or Ofsted) now assesses each one on how the idea of cultural capital is woven through the whole curriculum. The school inspection system defines *cultural capital* like this: "The essential knowledge that pupils need to be educated citizens, introducing them to the best that has been thought and said and helping to engender an appreciation of human creativity and achievement."[2]

Increasing cultural capital throughout a school curriculum aims to expose children to parts of life that are outside of their own experience and to enable them to understand the world a little bit better. There is a huge drive within modern education to reduce and even eradicate inequality; improving an individual student's cultural capital is now actively promoted as a way of doing this. Educational researchers and policy makers are asking questions about why children from deprived backgrounds often achieve less academically than their more privileged counterparts, and they are seeking solutions through a more equitable exposure to culture. In a traditional school setting this means more than just teaching children about a wider variety of arts, literature, and music. It is about broadening a student's opportunities to explore new cross-curricular activities, engage in social clubs, serve in the community, and even meet people from different backgrounds and generations. It means prioritising school trips to theatres, museums, areas of natural beauty, and places of interest that provide opportunities for questioning, curiosity, and creative social expression. Although there is an emerging recognition in British educational theory that spiritual, social, moral, and cultural investment makes a positive difference, it is fair to say that many UK teachers will report finding it difficult to fit these aspirational ideals into an already overstretched curriculum.

Decades before Bourdieu, Hirsch, and Ofsted, Charlotte Mason was writing and speaking to parents and educators about the importance of children connecting with great thought and creativity beyond themselves. In Victorian Britain there was an evident tension between the kind of education (and the expected outcome) of children of different classes. Charlotte desired for all children, even if they had limited resources, to have access to living books, time in nature, and exposure to beautiful works of art, literature, and music. She was a pioneer investor in cultural capital.

Making Investments in Culture

Capital is a word normally associated with economic investing. We can invest and build up cultural capital with our children through deposits, not of banknotes or stocks and shares, but via the currencies of art, poetry, music, theatre, and other forms of creative and literary expression. These things are not always spontaneous areas of interest for our twenty-first-century teenagers; many are devoid of the currency of culture and beauty unless an adult has opened the doorway for them in early life. That's where we as parents need to help our children prioritise exposure to culture.

Charlotte taught that "thought breeds thought."[3] If we want our children to think for themselves and to be creative and inventive, we must introduce them to people of great thought and creativity. Charlotte went as far to say that if you give your child a single valuable idea, "you have done more for his education than if you had laid upon his mind the burden of bushels of information."[4] So, if we want to foster a sense of cultural interest and imagination in childhood, then we might start by defining what we mean when we say we want to introduce them to "the best that has been thought and said."[5]

The 2003 film *Mona Lisa Smile*, starring Julia Roberts, depicts a timeless example of how educational institutions have limited our thinking around art and beauty. Roberts's character, Professor Katherine Ann Watson, leads a class of 1950s traditional upper-class schoolgirls into a warehouse to view a large Jackson Pollock painting before it goes on formal display. She invites them to look at the painting as an example of modern art in contrast to the classics they are used to encountering.

Whilst many of the students are following Miss Watson's invitation to absorb the manic, textured, black-and-grey brushstrokes on the deeply expressive piece of canvas, one slightly obnoxious girl pipes up, "Please don't tell me we have to write a paper about it." At this point the teacher turns to the class and says, "Do me a favour; do yourselves a favour: stop talking and look. You're not required to write a paper. You're not even required to like it. You are required to consider it. That's your only assignment today; when you're done, you may leave."[6]

This is what the heart of investing in cultural capital is about. Children do not always have to write about it, they probably won't be tested on it in an exam, and they don't even have to love it; they just need to consider what we expose them to. We are inviting our children to see or experience something new and decide for themselves if it is worthy to add onto their own *best of* list.

Charlotte's ideas take children away from the smallness of classrooms and grades and open a doorway to a lifetime of learning and connection full of rich exposure to culture. Her methods lead students to a place of consideration of beauty, not to a place where they are restricted by a syllabus and testing. The best of thoughts come to us through living books and experiences of all varieties, from ancient Plutarch to the modern-day nature insights of John Muir Laws. When we help children to connect with art, music, poetry, and plays, it heightens and increases what Charlotte referred to as their "Beauty Sense."[7] And beauty sense is what is required for us to truly grasp living insight. Charlotte described us all as having the "need to be trained to see, and to have our eyes opened before we can take in the joy that is meant for us in this beautiful life."[8] It would therefore be dismissive of us to regard our children's exposure to art, poetry, or classical music as additional sideline extras.

In Charlotte's fourth volume in the Home Education series, *Ourselves* (which is two books in one), she delves into the inner workings of the mind, describing it in such an illustrative way as "galleries" laden with pictures, poems, and perfectly placed ideas. As I read Susanna Clarke's intriguing novel *Piranesi* recently, I was thrown back into a similar picture of halls, corridors, and rooms—rooms full of mystery and intrigue but providing solace and a gentle escape from the world. As the narrator describes the landscape of his environment:

> In my mind are all the tides, their seasons, their ebbs and their flows. In my mind are all the halls, the endless procession of

them, the intricate pathways. When this world becomes too much for me, when I grow tired of the noise and the dirt and the people, I close my eyes and I name a particular vestibule to myself; then I name a hall.[9]

So, if our children's minds really are a maze of halls and galleries, we have a responsibility to ensure they aren't filled haphazardly by coincidence or default. We can help carefully curate their mind galleries as we lead them into places of continual beauty and expose them to culture in their learning days. I wonder what our children will hang in the galleries of their minds.

Making Cultural Investments in Experiences

Engaging with cultural beauty, especially within education, is a multisensory experience. Charlotte exhorted us that children must actively hear music and birdsong, look at art, admire and immerse themselves in nature, and read and recite poetry. These components spark the intellect and are a catalyst to conversation and a means to curate creative memories. Learning is meant to be a whole body, whole mind, and whole person experience!

One summer's day a couple of years ago, my husband and I took our younger children to Stratford-upon-Avon to an outdoor presentation of various monologues from Shakespeare's plays. Now, my children had been exposed to Shakespeare from a young age, delving into Edith Nesbit's *Beautiful Stories from Shakespeare*, followed by Charles and Mary Lamb's *Tales from Shakespeare*, before moving on to the plays themselves. The children were dubious at first; it was hot, and we had to sit on the ground, but as Micah found shade under a tree and Sienna snuggled in next to me with a cap on her head and sunscreen liberally applied, I soon saw the grins appear. The medieval-style music, the lively expressive actors, and some of the familiar lines and phrases they had learnt lit up their minds and their faces. This holistic experience of seeing and experiencing Shakespeare had them singing "Hey, Nonny, Nonny" from *Much Ado about Nothing* all the way home! We had read, listened to recordings, and watched BBC filmed versions of the plays, but nothing beat an original outdoor theatre experience akin to what we imagine the early performances were like in the late 1500s.

These multidimensional encounters may seem like they are not always frequently accessible or even consistently affordable, but they can make all the difference. It is all about making learning tangible. A trip to a farm or zoo can take a study on mammals to the next level. A conversation with a veteran might bring the struggles of history to life. A play reenacted at home with each person playing a different character can foster empathy, expression, and depth. We don't just have to learn about something; we can make learning come alive through a hands-on experience of sights, sounds, and smells.

Think of it like the difference between teaching nature purely from books and field guides in the confines of our four walls as opposed to taking children outside. Only outside can they feel the bark of a tree, allow a green shield beetle to walk on their hand, or merely smell the roses. Culture must be experienced, and not just read about, if it is to be remembered. And even if children can only read about certain aspects of culture for a period, they must experience those aspects through discussion, questioning, processing, or even physically acting them out in some way, to enable them to take ownership and claim the knowledge for themselves.

Making Cultural Investments in Art

Classical musician, author, and BBC Radio 3 presenter Clemency Burton-Hill was at the prime of her life, living in New York City with her family, when her life changed forever. In January 2020 at the age of thirty-nine, right before the onslaught of the global pandemic, she underwent sudden emergency brain surgery after collapsing from a brain haemorrhage. Clemency's recovery has been captured by major newspapers, radio broadcasts, and podcast interviews, where they have reported that music has played a key role in her radical recovery. As I've followed her story across the various forms of media, I've been struck by her return to enjoyment of art and music, even before she had full use of speech or physical movement. In the midst of her early recovery, she reported on her Instagram account a story of her return to the reopened Metropolitan Museum of Art:

> But there it was. The Met reopened, albeit in a limited capacity. Thousands upon thousands of years of human beings, making art, for no reason and yet every reason. I will defend to the end the idea that humans, all humans, need—deserve?—this. For explanation, for beauty, for wonderment, for hope. Especially for hope. Especially now.[10]

Art is not just for viewing but for investing our souls in. It reminds us of hope and what life is worth living for. Artists remind us to thrive and not just survive.

It is fascinating to me that Clemency herself comes from a line of people bringing hope and beauty to the world. Her father, Humphrey Burton, was the head of BBC Music and the Arts. He set out on a mission to bring the arts into the audience's living room through the medium of television. When Burton's autobiography was released, one commenter on Clemency's Instagram account had this to say: "As a working-class Eastender whose parents couldn't afford to attend concerts or theatre or really buy records, we devoured all the TV programmes he created. . . . They led to my lifelong love of classical music, opera, theatre, and art."[11] Making deposits in our cultural capital really is for everyone.

Art is an expression of beauty, a reflection of humanity, and a peek into history. Plato believed that the arts were powerful shapers of character, able to stir up emotions and influence our behaviour. We often naively come to art with the idea that we're supposed to have a clear opinion to like it or loathe it, or even decide that we could do it better ourselves! When we introduce children to beauty, we are simply asking them to look, just like they'd look at a beautiful view in the countryside, gaze at an ocean sunset, or wonder at Disney's Magic Kingdom light show. We're not asking them to critique, appreciate, overanalyse, or even analyse at all. We're just asking them to look at pieces of art, then at the right time, tell us what they saw, felt, or experienced—giving them agency in their experience. We're inviting them in to approach any picture or painting however they like, even allowing them to dislike it—and to communicate all that comes up in them whilst looking.

I usually ask my children to look over a piece of art for two or three minutes in silent reflection, gazing deep into the background, foreground, faces, and spaces for the whole time. I then take the painting away and simply say, "Tell me what you saw." I've done group sessions with children of all ages, and even though we don't ask the four-year-olds to "tell back," their perspective and attention to detail (which of course they are dying to share) is fascinating. What I love is the difference of perspective with each child, and especially with each age. In one session with my younger children, we were looking at a piece by Raphael called *Saint Catherine of Alexandria*. In the bottom left-hand corner of the painting there is a tiny image of a dandelion flower seed head. It was really hard to see, but of course, my keen-eyed daughter spotted it. This piqued our curiosity, so we started to research the painting further online. We then discovered that the dandelion seed painted in the picture was very significant in its time and was most likely representative of Christian grief and the Passion (Christ's torture and crucifixion). Pausing for the details started an unexpected spiritual conversation for the encouragement of our souls.

Young children approach the world with wide eyes and hospitable hearts; they are intrigued by our excitement and enthusiasm and can often be found to follow suit, especially when it comes to art. My young nieces were at my house, and in typical "Auntie Leah" style we painted pictures, followed by a nature walk in the park. The three-year-old took a whole pile of paper and was enthusiastically painting a squiggle on one piece, then moving on to another piece. I didn't want to squash her creative flair and ask her to "stop wasting paper," but I was slightly concerned our supply was rapidly running low. Next to where she was working in our homeschool room, the wall displayed various Munch, Cézanne, and Raphael prints and postcards. I caught her attention, pointed to the paintings on the wall and said, "Hey look, these are done by artists like you, and the paper is full of wonderful colour and squiggles and swirls." She took in what I said and triumphantly filled a whole page with a picture of her "daddy" with swirling colour all around him. Her slightly older sister was watching and listening in whilst drawing a beautiful picture of a flower; as she finished, she proudly explained how she'd filled the page with lines of colour, just like the artists. Even in just a short snippet of time, we can gently encourage, letting an example do its work to grow a child's creativity and connection.

Dr. Susie Nyman was a guest on the *Modern Miss Mason* podcast during an early season. Our paths first crossed whilst speaking at an online conference. I was the keynote speaker and was hosting a workshop about Charlotte Mason. She was sharing from her work with children with special educational needs and equipping parents with practical ideas for teaching. During our digital interactions she made me aware, almost in passing, that she actually attended a PNEU school (the Parents' National Educational Union institution founded by Charlotte Mason) back in the 1960s. I knew immediately I had to talk to her more about this! Dr. Susie painted a fascinating picture of her rich school days filled with nature study, art appreciation, science experiments, and great books. She then told me one striking story about how as an adult she had visited the Louvre in Paris with friends. As they were wandering around the galleries, she found herself naming the artist and even some of the titles of the paintings. Her travel companions were in awe of her knowledge and kept asking, "How do you know all these?" to which she replied, "I'm not sure; it's just all in my mind—must be from school." Susie told me about how she and her classmates had studied the masters, and despite her going on to work in education, these paintings have hung in her mind gallery forever.

I discovered only recently that my grandfather was a budding artist, and he used to fill my mother's childhood home with his own work. The result of this influence was that my mum, as an adult homeowner herself, would buy famous pieces of art or cut them out of calendars and hang them around the house. She wouldn't make us look at them or even tell us who the artists were; they were just present in our home. Many of them turned out to be Renoir—she loved his depictions of romantic-looking French ladies in their lovely clothes. I didn't know much about these paintings, but when there's a huge Renoir hanging on the back of your bathroom door, you can't help but imprint that on your memory!

Whilst on a trip to Paris to celebrate my daughter Nyah's sixteenth birthday together with my mother, we visited the wonderful Musée d'Orsay. My mum and I linked arms as we admired the paintings, the colours, the light, and the atmosphere. As we walked around the corner together, there on the wall was a painting, large as life and thick with paint—it was Renoir's *Dance at Bougival*. Tears came in my eyes as I gasped and said, "Mum, that's a picture from my childhood, the one in the bathroom."

"Yes," she said, "and that one, and that one too" (pointing to many others around the room). That walk around the gallery taking in Renoir and Monet originals was not just a Parisian highlight but a true trip down memory lane. It shows how the simple seeds of art and beauty sown in my childhood still grow in me today.

My father tells stories of his 1960s school years in Leeds, Yorkshire: he remembers lining up to attend the morning assembly, where, as they walked into the hall, classical music played through the speakers and famous art prints were hung on the walls. He doesn't recall studying them, or even teachers making a learning opportunity from them; they were just part of the atmosphere of the school. I wonder if we can so easily overcomplicate adding these elements to our children's lives, when mere exposure for eyes and ears can capture a child's heart and create memories to be drawn upon in the years to come.

Charlotte valued what paintings and compositions represent. Our children are not only paying attention to the direction of light or the sweeping motion of the artist's paintbrush, they are entering into an artist's or musician's life. Researching that life is not a prerequisite to admiring creativity, but I find that personal story or biography adds another dimension to our experience with their work. The story of a picture marks it out from the rest and makes it valuable. After all, it is wondering what lies behind Mona Lisa's smile that keeps the crowds coming to see it year upon year. Creators' lives don't always end positively (Van Gogh's ear, anyone?), so when it comes to researching the lives of the artists we've chosen, I certainly delve in first before sharing with my children! Yet even when art history reveals a darker past for us, it can still provide opportunities to explore spiritual, moral, or social questions.

I've always admired Mary Oliver's poetry. As soon as I was introduced to it many years ago, I endeavoured to read and engage with her work as much as possible. Oliver didn't appear on social media, nor was she interviewed by hundreds of podcast hosts during a book launch; it seemed that her work did the promoting for her. However, on one occasion, legendary interviewer Krista Tippett managed to get a treasured interview with Oliver a few years before she died, on Tippett's popular podcast *On Being*—much to Oliver's fans' delight. I've listened to this interview time and time again as it reveals so much depth, yet simplicity, about her life; and this only deepens my love for her writing. The story of her poetry now weaves with the story of her life. Learning about any artist only enriches the power of the art itself.

Making Cultural Investments in Music

I grew up in a home full of music. My dad played guitar and practised almost daily. My mum has a beautiful singing voice, and being the happiest person I know, she sang around the house a lot. My parents would play various genres; I'd wake up to anything from Gregorian chants, to lively charismatic worship music, to Vivaldi's *Four Seasons*. I was familiar with varying styles of music and would find the low hum of a CD playing in our dining room particularly comforting. My dad would regularly ask us questions about what we were listening to, such as "What instruments can you hear in this piece of music?" as Benjamin Britten's *Young Person's Guide to the Orchestra* sounded out from our 1980s music system. The idea of playing music, whether classical or any other variety, to my children came naturally to me. Playing Mozart to our womb-bound young was quite trendy in the early 2000s, as the Baby Einstein brand was growing. I sat my children in front of books and videos that had stimulating shapes and colours accompanied by classical music. We were told via popular science that early years' behaviour of this kind would boost our child's IQ, and of course we all aspired to have smart kids. Whilst evidence shows listening to classical music doesn't directly improve an individual's IQ, it has been found to have many benefits, from boosting memory to aiding relaxation.[12]

I can't quite imagine what Charlotte would think of listening to

Baby Einstein, as she came to include music appreciation in her pro-grammes much later in her journey. The inspiration came to her after hearing how her friend and colleague Mrs. Glover played music to her own children. Mrs. Glover remembers the instance and recalled it dur-ing an address she made at the Ambleside Conference in 1922, during which she said, "[Charlotte] realised that music might give great joy and interest to the life of all, and she felt that just as children in the P.U.S. [Parent Union Schools] were given the greatest literature and art, so they should have the greatest music as well."[13]

The addition of music appreciation is about fostering relationships with the lives of those who created the music. We can approach this element, as with picture study or the regular reading of poetry, and build up a knowledge, appreciation, and familiarity with the work of one composer. As our children listen day after day to familiar tunes of beauty and depth, they are forming opinions, tastes, and memories that they'll draw upon one day in the most unexpected places.

The soundtrack of our homeschooling days must now represent our modern lives. I love to create monthly playlists brimming with jazz, classical music, gospel, folk, and worship songs to fill our home with atmosphere. Let's not be limited to the gramophone classics of bygone years, but we should allow our children to listen in on the sounds of the past as they learn to also appreciate the music and arts of today. This might mean discussing a line about the Lake District ("Take me to the lakes where all the poets went to die") in a song hidden on a Taylor Swift album. Or it might mean making the connection between the latest Marvel movie signature theme and the classic composer's magnum opus it alludes to. What matters is not the genre, style, or artist, nor the apparent worthiness of the piece. It matters not if it is on an approved curriculum list but rather what it means to you and your family. Does your world seem slightly better, brighter, or a little bigger because of what you have seen, heard, or experienced?

We have a visceral connection to music that is powerful. It can remain even when other parts of our body or brain are failing us. There is a theory that musical memories are often preserved longer because certain areas of the brain can be relatively undamaged by terrible conditions like Alzheimer's. My sister-in-law tells the story of her mother, who suffered with dementia in her final years; she couldn't remember who most family members were or most memories of her life, but as soon as my brother and his wife began to sing hymns when they visited her in the residential home, she remembered them all and joined in. This reminded me of a video I saw online that featured a female Alzheimer's patient who, in her younger years, was a prima ballerina and frequently performed *Swan Lake*. The patient sat in a wheelchair and was given a pair of headphones to wear. As the sound in her ears played Tchaikovsky's *Swan Theme*, she was transported as if back into the body of her younger self and began the graceful arm movements of the dance.[14] This incredibly moving scene demonstrates the power of musical memories that are held in the mind and body.

My granddad lived until he was ninety-two years old. In his final few years, he was in a nursing home in West Yorkshire, and I visited him on a few occasions. The last time I saw my granddad, he was lying in a bed, physically quite weak, but his mind was quick and alert. During these visits I often told him of the composers and artists our family were engaging with, and on this day he related a story from his childhood. He began to reflect on being nine years old and on a "date" with a girl! They went to see a film at the cinema, and whilst on the way home he made up a song to the tune of one of Dvořák's classical *Humoresques*. As he told the story, he began to sing the words to his made-up song whilst giggling at how silly they were. Sitting beside his bed, I asked my granddad if he'd like to hear a version of his favourite piece of music right then. Of course, he said yes, so I opened YouTube on my phone and found an orchestral version for him. As the music played, Granddad hummed along to the tune like a gleeful child, without a single note missed. With tears in his eyes, he gently held my hand, even as tears streamed down my face too. As his body was laid to rest in the summer of 2019, his loving, loyal sons arranged for Dvořák's *Humoresque* to be the last piece of music played. This piece is now incredibly meaningful to me, not because it was on a curriculum or a recommended list, and not only as a legacy of my grandfather's life, but because it is a reminder that a familiar tune can be woven throughout one's story forever.

Every generation needs someone to lead the way, to pull back the curtains and introduce children and young people to the beauty found in art and culture. Now, in the twenty-first century we have no excuses; we have concerts in the palm of our hands, and art at our fingertips. We only need to open the door wide and show generous hospitality to the ideas and contribution of the younger generation. And if the cultural capital we build up in our children's lives really will stay deep in their souls, even to the end of their days, then surely it is worth making sure what we offer them daily will stand the test of time.

TAKE A MASON MOMENT:
Suggestions for Cultivating Culture in the Home

- Keep art handy. Next time you're at an art gallery, buy a handful of art print postcards; these might not be used for your "formal" picture study, but have them around to hold, flick through, or display on the walls.
- Build up a playlist of classical music tracks that you've seen or heard your children respond to (e.g., galloping around to Rossini's *William Tell Overture*). Have a classical radio station playing quietly as children are waking up and starting their day.

- Find out what artists are featured in your local art gallery, or one you can access easily—study them, then visit the pieces in real life.
- Use a tablet or laptop to access art online; you can get up close and personal, zooming in on details that you'd rarely see from a print or postcard.
- Try to integrate poetry as a regular rhythm; read it aloud, listen to podcast recordings, try out author-read audiobook versions. Poetry is written to be spoken aloud and sounded out on the lips.
- Keep a notebook of first impressions when engaging with all forms of the arts, asking the question "What did you think of . . . ?" This is interesting to look back on and see how ideas around art, music, poetry, and plays have developed over the years.
- Do a picture study. Look at any art for a set time. Then ask the child to recall what they have seen as the beginning of a conversation.
- Plan regular real-life field trips (even if they are free) that will help bring any given topic to life.
- Invent a creative experiential way for your child to engage their five senses (sight, sound, smell, taste, and touch) within any subject.
- Listen to a variety of genres of music; I create a monthly playlist that we listen to most mornings as we're starting the day together. These can consist of hymns, folk songs, classical, jazz, gospel, etc. Keep it varied, interesting, and lively!
- Copy art, play music, write poems, and act out scenes. Children will be inspired by the creators they are learning from. Let's give them an opportunity to express that.

- Go to a concert if you can, or watch one online—this is a great way to see instruments being played and enjoy the conductor shaping the sequence of music.
- Use map work to complement what you are reading or learning. Download blank or labelled maps and use them to locate where countries are or to discuss what kind of culture they have.
- Take your learning to a new location for the day. A simple change of scenery can open new learning possibilities together.

Part 3

Reframing Motherhood

Chapter 9

Creating Soul Space

*If mothers could learn to do for themselves
what they do for their children when these are overdone,
we should have happier households.
Let the mother go out to play!*
CHARLOTTE MASON, *SCHOOL EDUCATION*

*Though Charlotte Mason wasn't a mother herself, she worked closely
with countless mothers, observing their tenacity, powerful nurturing
abilities, and their endless, selfless work. She noticed a correlation
between how refreshed the mothers were and their ability to trust
childhood and the educational methods she taught. To help get the
best outcome for the children she sent mothers out to play!*

Recapturing Our Spirit of Playfulness

Children seem to have no trouble inventing endless ways to play. They
are often fully able to entertain themselves with vivid, expressive games
from their own imaginations without the encouragement or supervision of adults. In fact, adults can arguably be the disrupters rather than
instigators of a child's play. The sound of a child laughing and playing
is so often a balm for the mother's soul because it reminds us of a lost
art that we long to find in our present moment.

Charlotte believed in parents so much (and really wanted us to do a great job) that she designed an extensive programme of input and introspection called the Mothers' Education Course. This involved guidance and teaching in faith, health, educational philosophy, and nature. The formal course didn't survive much past the First World War due to the changing priorities of women; but the principles it explored still ring true today in our book clubs, forums, social media pages, live videos, and the many research bodies that continue sharing her work.

The mission of motherhood and the toll on our bodies, minds, and time hasn't changed much over the past one hundred years. There are so many factors to consider when it comes to our approach to free time, relaxation, and self-management, but I don't think anyone can argue that it's not important. We are living in the most fast-paced, stressed-out society ever. Mothers are expected to "bounce back," run a business from home with a baby on the hip, and meet every need for anything that breathes or moves in her household! Slowing down and giving our minds and bodies what they need can often seem indulgent, rather than a source of health and longevity. After personally fighting such thoughts over the years, I have finally taken the long road to slowing down and savouring every given opportunity.

In an article by the *Washington Post* entitled "Why It's Good for Grown-ups to Go Play," psychiatrist Stuart Brown talks about the effects of the lack of play in our adult lives. The article reports,

> "Play is a basic human need as essential to our well-being as sleep, so when we're low on play, our minds and bodies notice," Brown says. Over time, he says, play deprivation can reveal itself in certain patterns of behavior: We might get cranky, rigid, feel stuck in a rut or feel victimized by life. To benefit most from the rejuvenating benefits of play, he says,

we need to incorporate it into our everyday lives, "not just wait for that two-week vacation every year."[1]

Playing contributes to a healthy mind, body, and spirit and is known to boost our confidence and self-esteem. It forges positive relationships and connections, triggers our problem-solving skills, and stimulates creative thinking. It keeps us functioning well under stress and releases endorphins that help us cope. Play is not just an activity but a state of mind. It reminds us to be less intense and not take ourselves too seriously. It doesn't take much of a mental leap to recognise how much this kind of attitude and approach to life can have a positive effect on our children and in our home. It turns out that fun is a serious business that is worthy of our effort.

Charlotte's idea of play for mothers wasn't merely intended to give us time off; it was about fueling us for the noble job we are undertaking. Play takes our focus off feeling responsible and weighed down with work; it awakens our intellect, provokes our sense of wonder, and refreshes our souls. Play gives us a fresh perspective, guards us from idolising our role or our children, and enables us to recognise that we're still growing, changing, and taking part in the world.

Dealing with Our Barriers to Play

Whilst short-term practical excuses such as tiredness or busyness often cause us to delay our play, it is perhaps the long-term psychological barriers that most frequently prevent us from taking time to play. We can often feel that we are not fulfilling our motherly duties if we take time out and even worry that we are being reckless to prioritise such childish endeavours. We become self-conscious as we compare ourselves with the seemingly more productive types who can do it all, and we fail to give ourselves permission for fun.

I unknowingly did this in my early years of home educating my children.

I came into the home educating life somewhat confidently. I had idealistic views from the books and the blogs I'd read which convinced me that teaching my children at home would result in endlessly inspiring, shiny, and perfect lives for the whole family. The problem with having fixed ideals rather than a clear vision is that they can undermine our own decisions when we don't live up to these expectations. It is not about having low expectations but rather guarding ourselves from false ones. We can't keep attempting to live someone else's homeschool journey if we are going to embrace our own. Part of my personal journey into Charlotte Mason's notion of play was to first recognise the impact of comparison and false expectations, then adjust my habits and priorities accordingly.

Our exertion of generous giving inevitably leads us to need replenishment. Charlotte's encouragement for mothers to "play" may have been a progressive concept for Victorian mothers, yet modern society is overly familiar with terms such as "self-care" and "me time," and we have a myriad of escapist pastimes at our literal fingertips to take our minds off what is hard. There can be a temptation to zone out and lose ourselves in entertainment rather than tune in to find ourselves through engaged play.

Our lives are bombarded by ways to implement self-care into our days; these may consist of luxury products poured into a bath, delectable edibles wrapped in gold foil, or a manicure experienced in peace and quiet. Whilst there's nothing wrong with these lovely additions to life, they're not always practical or accessible to a busy mother. An awareness or concern for ourselves is important but must not be confined to our exterior lives: it must also look inward. This care for the inner workings of our soul plays out in so many areas of our lives, from the way we manage our daily responsibilities through to how we treat other people. Charlotte reminds us that our power to conduct our relationships with other people depends upon our power to conduct our relationship with ourselves.

Investing in my inner life and taking time to fuel my mind and soul have been a guard and protection for me in times of stress and conflict. It has been a place to draw from when parenting has pushed every button and my children's choices haven't quite lined up with mine! Knowing that I am also a born person, someone of value, and that I am worth giving the gift of time, words, and creativity has been an anchor over the many years of raising and educating my children.

Embracing the Challenge to Play

Charlotte Mason was a woman who was no stranger to hardship. Orphaned as a teenager and forced to find her own way in the world, she arrived at the teaching career she had dreamed of from when she was a young girl. She worked hard but had a grey cloud of illness constantly hanging over her, right through her life. Though she wasn't a biological mother, Charlotte walked alongside many "bairns," as she referred to her students. She was a friend to so many, and she was the mother of a revolutionary educational movement. Although Charlotte may not have been able to relate to the pain of childbirth or the weight of responsibility mothers feel when raising their own children, she did experience loss, hardship, and struggle that gave her insight into the power of caring for oneself. Her constant work with parents and her interaction with children also gave her a bird's-eye view of a mother's longing and need for refreshment as she pours herself out into her children.

When I first came to understand Charlotte's work and words, I was reminded of a story from the Bible. Isaac's father, Abraham, had dug some wells, but their enemies plugged them up, so Isaac redug the wells and renamed them.[2] This act stemmed from Isaac's desire to reconnect with his history, restore his personal roots, and perhaps even recapture some of his heritage. Yet this task was met with so much quarrelling, arguing, and confusion at the first few wells that Isaac was disappointed by the mission he set out on and almost gave up. Digging deep is often harder than it looks.

Yet after persisting onwards, Isaac had a breakthrough. The Bible says that "he moved from there and dug another well, and they did not quarrel over it. So he called its name Rehoboth, because he said, 'For now the LORD has made room for us, and we shall be fruitful in the land.'"[3] *Rehoboth* means a spacious place (it is what we have named our home), and I think that this word beautifully describes a Charlotte Mason education. An education built on this foundation is spacious, generous, and continuous. Rehoboth is a wide-open place where we as mothers, parents, and educators can move freely, a place where we can be fruitful and grow. But it is a place we must fight for, one that life will contest unless we determine to keep digging. Whilst working for Rehoboth even the hardiest of mothers can grow weary. But I love how Charlotte said that mothers will always "work wonders once they are convinced that wonders are demanded of them!"[4]

Our view of motherhood determines how much we prioritise play. Early on in my mothering journey a wise, much older homeschool hero said this to me: "It's not enough to just love your children, you must also learn to love motherhood." Through this advice I began to see motherhood as a noble calling, something I was fully equipped to do beautifully and uniquely; something I would choose to hold lightly but navigate with integrity and intentionality. Once we know what we are digging deeply for, it is worth taking the continual challenge to stay alive in our learning, pursue masterly inactivity around our children, and keep our souls well watered.

Learning to Play Again

So how do we start to play? This can be a hugely challenging question to answer, but this is where the creativity of mothers is wonderful. Start by creating a list of activities that delight your soul yet rest your body. Don't wait until you're collapsing and at the end of your tether, as we say here in England, but rather schedule play as part of your planned calendar. Talk to your family about having at least an hour a week away from responsibilities, a time period which will hopefully increase as your children grow older. Drink your favourite tea, take a walk in the park, sit and listen to the birds, stare at art (I have a print by my desk at all times), journal for yourself, and read poetry aloud—the list can be endless when we actually take time to make it.

The full excerpt at the start of this chapter is probably the most oft-quoted part of Charlotte's work, but I'm convinced it takes years to fully learn the vital place of it and the significance of its regularity in our lives. It takes time and dedication to fully appreciate the power of play talked about here:

> If mothers could learn to do for themselves what they do
> for their children when these are overdone, we should have
> happier households. Let the mother go out to play! If she
> would only have courage to let everything go when life
> becomes too tense, and just take a day, or half a day, out in
> the fields, or with a favourite book, or in a picture gallery
> looking long and well at just two or three pictures, or in bed,
> *without the children*, life would go on far more happily for
> both children and parents. The mother would be able to hold
> herself in "wise passiveness," and would not fret her children
> by continual interference, even of hand or eye—she would
> let them be.[5]

In this encouragement we can draw out several practical suggestions from Charlotte worth integrating into our daily lives. We can relax our mind, rewind in nature, read a book, receive from creativity, and refresh our body.

Relaxing Your Mind

All over the world, leading voices in mental and emotional well-being are guiding us to lead healthier lifestyles. We are more aware than ever before of the impact of stress and anxiety upon our lives and the lives of those around us. As mothers we are not exempt from these pressures.

Charlotte advises us to "let everything go when life becomes too tense." No one is immune to life becoming tense, and there truly is wisdom in just walking away at times (physically or metaphorically) to get some fresh perspective. I have done this on countless occasions; it's usually a case of "I need to sleep, then everything will look/feel different afterwards." It may take an intentional conversation with a spouse, a partner, a friend, or a relative to make this work in reality, but please, dear mother, give it a go.

There are so many methods and maps to mindfulness, but the key is to give space for your mind to rest, as well as your body. I relate to the writer Shauna Niequist who talks about "fake-rest" in her book *Present over Perfect*. This concept refers to the idea that everyone else in your family can be taking time out, watching television, playing games, and lazing around in all the best ways, but whilst you may appear to have stopped outwardly, you are inwardly still going at a million miles per hour in your mind. As Shauna says, "I fake-rested instead of real-rested, and then I found that I was real-tired. It feels ludicrous to be a grown woman, a mother, still learning how to rest."[6]

Ludicrous or not, I have had to learn that there is a difference between real recovery and rest. Recovery is the time it takes to get yourself back to zero after a time of exertion. Rest is what fills you above the line. The root of this is permission and discipline. We must give ourselves permission to fully rest and discipline ourselves not just to practise a sit-and-scroll-with-your-phone kind of rest, but the kind of deep playfulness that rejuvenates you from the inside out and makes you feel human again!

One more note: I am no expert nor qualified whatsoever to speak into the area of mental health, but I know that there is a difference between feeling under pressure and being totally overwhelmed and helpless. When the stresses you face leave you feeling unable to function or cope, then it is time to be honest and ask for help. I hope, if you are reading this today and are struggling with your mental health, that you'd reach out for help where you can and know that you are still valued, worthy, and loved.

Rewinding in Nature

Charlotte loved to travel (and due to ill health, often had to journey for respite and healing bath treatment). She also built into her daily life frequent walks or carriage rides through the rambling hills of the Lake District to see what was in bloom, collect wildflowers to display at her school (called Scale How), or simply to hear the birds sing. She reclined on her blue sofa with a volume of Sir Walter Scott near at hand, and I'm sure her mind was ablaze with the conversations and observations from the day. Her faithful companion Elsie Kitching records for *In Memoriam* "She never worked out of hours nor let herself think of problems at night."[7] Now, that must have taken true self-discipline and self-permission to execute.

Charlotte's advice to "just take a day, or half a day, out in the fields" can be a balm to a weary mother. A walk in the woods, a stroll through the park, or dipping your toes in the local river can jolt your emotions into a more relaxed state, enabling you to think more clearly and act calmer. Feeling revived and refreshed by nature is not a modern phenomenon; poets and writers over the centuries have directed us out-doors to let nature be our teacher. The peaceful hum of grasshoppers, a wren singing in a treetop, and the lapping of the ocean against rocks is literal "music to our ears," thus soothing our soul. It's easy to tick off our personal nature exposure with the school-day nature walks, but let me encourage you to create space for that solo time out in the fields when you can.

Reading a Book

The Parents' Review was a monthly magazine dedicated to home-training and culture which was edited by Charlotte Mason until she died. In a well-known article titled "Mother Culture," published in the late 1800s, the writer reflects on someone she met who inspired her to read more. I love this quaint story she tells:

> The wisest woman I ever knew—the best wife, the best mother, the best mistress, the best friend—told me once, when I asked her how, with her weak health and many calls upon her time, she managed to read so much. "I always keep three books going—a stiff book, a moderately easy book, and a novel, and I always take up the one I feel fit for!" That is the secret; always have something "going" to grow by.[8]

Those pursuing a Charlotte Mason education, in whatever shape or form, will know that books are a major component in what that education looks like. We find ourselves searching for, shopping for, and surrounded by beautiful books to line our children's academic lives. Yet no matter how incredible our child's read aloud is, it can never take the place of our own digging for knowledge by spending time "with a favourite book."

Just as the woman in the previous story, I like to break my reading down into a few different categories.

I read for devotion. Whether you are a person of faith or not, you can read to fuel your soul. For me this looks like daily Bible reading, but I also have a stack of books and poetry compilations that I'd file under "devotional." I keep them all in one place beside my favourite chair, alongside my journals, and I dip into them as and when I see fit.

I read for delight. I was an avid fiction reader as a child (weren't we all?), but as I got into university study, adulthood, and eventually parenting, nonfiction took over my shelves. Even in my early home educating days my novel-loving friends would regularly ask me, "What fiction are *you* reading, Leah?" and throw recommendations my way. Now I have at least one novel on the go all the time, often on Audible so I can listen when I'm cooking, driving alone, or cleaning up the kitchen. Fiction keeps us in story, awakens us to wonder, and stops us (me especially) from being so serious! Fiction is always a source of enriching conversation. For example, I found that Matt Haig's much acclaimed *The Midnight Library* not only lived up to its bestseller status, but it has also provided so much engaging conversation fodder with family and fellow fiction-reading friends along the way.

I read for depth. This is what the inspiring woman from the article meant as a "stiff book." Reading for depth means reading a book that stretches your concentration, imagination, vocabulary, and capacity for understanding. These I often read slowly, thoughtfully, and with a notebook in hand. Last month I finally started Dante's *Divine Comedy*, and I'm quite sure I'll still be reading it for depth when this book finally hits your hands!

I read for discovery. This often meets in the middle with reading for depth, but this is how I categorise books on educational theory, personal interest, hobbies, and research. Everything from Charlotte Mason's six Home Education volumes (which are always close at hand) through to Monty Don's *The Complete Gardener* would make the cut here.

You don't have to be ordered in your reading if you don't want to be. There are no rules to replenishing your soul with reading. All of these categories can be on the go at the same time, stacked or shelved in various places around the house and picked up whether you have a few minutes in the bathroom or a whole luxurious afternoon curled up on the couch.

Receiving from Creativity

In a rare child-free moment, a friend and I seized the day and jumped on a train to Birmingham to look "long and well at just two or three pictures" in the city art gallery before it closed in the global pandemic for what seemed like an age. We were adults adventuring alone, wandering the city streets with souls longing for art and beauty. Both of us were tired and weary from homeschooling, with lockdown restrictions that kept us from even exploring our own country for a while. But on this day, we had our coffee, no children, and an art gallery in our sight. This was our way to play; we quietly and quite emotionally wandered the museum halls and stopped to stare at Degas, Millay, Cassatt, and many more. We breathed in the beauty, history, and heritage right in front of our eyes. We didn't need a spa or a manicure; we didn't need to zone out on technology; our souls required refreshment, and we'd learnt the long, sweet way that a brief cultural experience would provide it.

I love Julia Cameron's encouragement in her book *The Artist's Way* to take a regular date with ourselves. She describes the concept of an artist date as "a once-weekly, festive, solo expedition to explore something that interests you. The artist date need not be overtly 'artistic'— think mischief more than mastery. Artist dates fire up the imagination. They spark whimsy. They encourage play. Since art is about the play of ideas, they feed our creative work by replenishing our inner well of images and inspiration."[9]

I heard a mother recently express how she felt bad for having these kinds of experiences on her own and always felt she should have a child or two with her on her trips, but I disagree! These are not a formal educational trip or necessarily for us to "learn" something, they are beauty for the eyes and food for the soul. They're a sacred moment to be alone with your observations, a reminder of your perspective, and the chance to pause where you see beauty and sense glory. These experiences are of course not limited to an art gallery; how about a theatre trip, a spoken word poetry open mic night, or a stroll through a sculpture park? The idea is to be alone, or maybe with another mother, and to encounter art and beauty to the measure of your heart, not to the limit of the time your toddler can manage!

Refreshing Your Body

Sleep is an essential function that allows our bodies and minds to recharge so that we feel refreshed and alert when we're awake. Good sleep helps the body remain healthy and can even guard against disease. Without enough sleep, the brain cannot function properly; we can't concentrate or process clearly. When Charlotte instructs us to nap alone ("in bed, without the children"), I'm not sure if she is making a reference to how many Victorian children slept in one bed together, or possibly a comment on co-sleeping with a breastfed baby after overhearing many an exhausted mother trying to manage family and teaching on disturbed sleep. But, whatever her specific reference, we could all do with a little more sleep in our lives. As young adults we can think we're invincible (I certainly did), burning the candle at both ends, believing we can handle "business as usual" and blurring the lines between work and play; but as we get older, our need for good, deep sleep becomes key to productive days! Whether it's getting to bed early, a sneaky afternoon nap, or a preplanned Saturday lie-in, prioritise getting those hours in when you can, and you'll see how the glorious benefits are endless.

Being a mother is all consuming. As much as we find delight and joy in our days caring for our children, we were already whole and growing before they came along. Don't forget who you are as an individual, above and beyond the role you play for others. Remember the passions you carried, the interests that led you to create tabs on your browser, or the hobbies that filled your bookshelves. Make room for your living, growing self, and allow your children to see the beauty and fulfilment in adult life. Everyone has their own unique version of what play looks like to them. If you can't even remember the last time you took part in a hobby, interest, or pastime that wasn't about achieving an outcome but rather enjoying the process, then maybe you need to rebalance. We need to be brave enough to have conversations with those around us to practically enable us to prioritise play.

I love author Julie Bogart's concept of *awesome adulting*, which she speaks about across her social media platforms and in her literary works. This idea is about continuing to build our own life of interest and fun, whilst setting an example to our children.

I'm grateful to have examples of this around me: my mother who took up rag rugging in her sixties; Juliet, my friend with seven children, who joined a local a cappella barbershop group; Lucy, who decided to take a course in herbal remedies whilst pioneering a new business selling natural candles and wax melts; my knitting friend, Holly, who took a year to learn about foraging whilst raising and educating four girls; and then there's my always inspiring friend Serena, who in her forties joined a "true life storytelling" group (I accompanied her to a competition in Birmingham which we both agreed she should have won!).

Fellow Brit and my online friend Eloise Rickman (author of

Extraordinary Parenting) recently shared with me her decision to return to university in her early thirties to do an MA in the sociology of childhood and children's rights. I know this example would sit beautifully in the next chapter, which is focused on being intellectually alive, but when I asked Eloise why she chose to do this now, she answered: "I decided to do it in part because I felt it would enrich and inform my work and writing, but also (this is a bit cheesy) it felt like such a gift to my twenty-one-year-old self who desperately wanted to do a master's but couldn't afford it."[10]

A perfect, soul-enriching gift indeed!

We are not only to be a picture of a sacrificial, loving life for others but also one of exuberance, fun, and freedom. Let's be awesome adults! Let's leave a trail of a life that children would like to emulate, discuss with friends, and write about in books in years to come. A life they knew wasn't easy, but a life full of forgiveness and second chances, a life that is fully alive, and full of continued growth, grit, and grace. A life where mothers go out to play. A life like yours.

TAKE A MASON MOMENT:
Suggestions for Cultivating Soul Space

- Make a list of the barriers you have in your life right now to cultivating soul space, and then think through strategies to overcome them.
- Talk to people in your family (immediate or otherwise) about how you can practically make play happen and why it is so important for everyone, not just you. It is okay to ask for help.
- Know what you love. Give yourself permission to make a list of things that you enjoy and help you relax. Recognise the activities that bring life as well as help you rest.

- Take a moment in the day when your children can see or experience you "playing." Let them see you reading, listening to your favourite music, or dancing in the kitchen.
- Shop your local bookshop or favourite online bookstore for books that bring delight; these might be novels, photographic coffee-table books, or recipe guides. These will form something to flick through or curl up and read if you've got five minutes or an hour.
- Visit your own bookshelf.
- Schedule time in your diary for rest and refueling—and stick to it. Even if you're resting at home, plan to make a luxurious coffee or steep a special tea.
- Choose an accountability friend—you can check on each other and make sure you're making time to rest and play.
- Look after your body; it's the only one you have.
- Go for a local walk and leave your phone at home. Listen, look, and absorb whilst eliminating the temptation to share!
- Log out of your social media account for a while, take the email app off your phone, or set up restricted timings in your settings. Protect your time.
- Buy your favourite flavour of yogurt, coffee creamer, or type of cheese when grocery shopping as an occasional treat—choose something just for you!
- Plan a nap (in bed), tell everyone that it's going to happen and when, turn off your phone, close the curtains, snuggle down, and enjoy.
- Make or create something just for fun. Bake, take photos, animate on the iPad, choreograph a dance, or write a poem. Do it, just because you can. The process *is* the outcome.

Chapter 10

Becoming
Intellectually Alive

We need not say one word about the necessity for living thought in the teacher;
it is only so far as he is intellectually alive that he can be effective
in the wonderful process which we glibly call "education."

CHARLOTTE MASON, *PARENTS AND CHILDREN*

Charlotte Mason reminds mothers to keep a rhythm of life that
helps us stay intellectually alive not just for the sake of formal study.
As parents and educators, we can prioritise lifelong learning for
ourselves and thus leave a lasting impression on our children.

Mothers Who Still Love Learning

Even though "mummy brain" may sound like a convenient excuse to
forget what you are supposed to be doing that day, it is a real condition
backed by scientific studies. The inability to remember a character's
name in a TV show, or why you thought it was a good idea to put
your keys in the fridge, is now a symptom backed up by neuroscience, the study of hormones, and the odd confused family member or
two. If you have ever been infected by the brain fog of the baby years,
then you will know it is not always possible to feel like you have it all

together. I still believe no mother should be expected to remember all their children's names all the time!

Even if your days (and nights) are temporarily limited to diaper changes, breastfeeding, and toddler chasing, the muscles of the mind are still eager to be stretched. It is good to remember, even when we are struggling to focus, that our learning didn't start with formal education, and it doesn't have to stop with the advent of parenting. The process of learning is happening all the time whether we notice it or not.

Growing up, I was a recovering shy girl who didn't particularly fit the mainstream education system or tick all its boxes. My own childhood memories are full of lively play, stories being read aloud, nature walks, bookshelves full of interesting reads, and classical music heard around the home. My hardworking engineering father and my mother—a free-spirited, creative, stay-at-home wife—raised us with love, attention, and room to grow. We were encouraged to complete our homework, look up unknown vocabulary in a dictionary, let conversations flow around the dinner table, and watch the BBC news to wrap up our day. Whilst this atmosphere instilled a love for learning that has always been a part of my life, academic achievement has not always come easily to me.

My tenacity at school enabled me to scrape the grades, giving me the ticket to move on and through the required system. I was the first person from my family to go to university. I didn't go particularly due to my academic ambition but rather because that was the normal thing for young people to do after taking formal exams. I took a combined degree which eventually whittled down to a major in sociology and a minor in English literature. During my first term I received an A on an essay on Shakespeare's *Othello*. I was overjoyed (and slightly shocked), assuming the lecturer was just being nice because I was new. I never found out whether that was true, but I also never received an A ever again.

University was a season when I was surrounded by fascinating, interesting faculty. I loved listening to their tales of research and anthropological discoveries. I was engaged and felt alive in my studies, yet for some reason, I wasn't quite achieving the outcome the institution expected of me at that stage of my learning.

A standout moment from my university experience was when an esteemed lecturer, a man full of good nature, wisdom, and intellect spoke some home truths to me. I walked into the echoey lecture theatre for my usual weekly meeting with him to discuss my dissertation; there were a few uncomfortable fold-down blue chairs placed near the podium where the lecturer presents, and Dr. Riches beckoned me to take a seat. After a bit of small talk and a flick through the section I'd been working on, he said these words:

"You know, Leah, you probably won't get a great degree classification. But you'll always do well in life. You're just that kind of person."

At first, I was offended and determined I would prove him wrong. But it turned out he was spot-on. I scraped a BA Honours degree classification, enabling me to graduate, but I didn't even attend the ceremony because I was off on a new adventure, already "doing well in life" in a leadership programme in the USA.

Four years later it was my husband's turn to graduate; I'd long disappointed my grandparents by not providing a graduation photo for them to display on their wall next to my cousin Gavin's, so I decided today was the day to rectify that! After Dave's parents had proudly taken pictures of their son in his university finery, I quietly said to Dave, "Take off the cap and gown, let me wear it." Without much dispute he obliged and wrapped his gown around me, then placed the cap on my head. I then said, "Please can you take a photo of me?" I posed, smiled large, and successfully managed to create a fake graduation snap!

To this day that photo is still hanging on my grandma's wall, in her Yorkshire home.

I'd always had a thirst for learning but had never been the academic, top-grades kind of girl. Instead, I was the wide-eyed observer of the world, a poet with secret scribbles in journals written on plane journeys. I was the reader in youth hostel beds by a night-light. I was a leader with ideas and dreams to travel. I was, and still am, in my lecturer's words, "that kind of person."

I know many mothers would say their real education didn't begin until they started teaching their children. It is amazing how much we retain when we must remember it for the benefit of others. The nature of academia can be exciting and wonderful to some, yet to so many mothers, including myself, it can be a daunting millstone that convinces us that we won't make the grade with teaching our children, because we didn't always make the grade ourselves. It is in this tension that we are reminded how important it is to prioritise becoming intellectually alive for both ourselves and our children's sake.

Charlotte had many intriguing contemporary educational influences, one prominent person being the poet and school inspector Matthew Arnold. One of Arnold's values for his teaching staff was to stay on a continuous learning journey themselves. He sent them away regularly to top up their qualifications or refresh their knowledge. Following in his steps, Charlotte implored her governesses, teachers, and mothers to stay "intellectually alive," this being particularly important when mothers were wholly responsible for facilitating their children's education.

Mothers Who Invest in Their Own Journey

One of the things I love to do is listen to podcasts or watch documentaries interviewing older women with interesting life stories. I recently listened to two podcast recordings, one interviewing the wonderful Dame Judi Dench, and another with the inimitable Julie Andrews. Both women are in the winter of their lives, with successful, well-respected careers as actors, directors, and authors. What stood out to me about these women is how they both commented that they never stopped learning. Their internal learning journeys were foundational to their external success. They individually talked of nurturing creative rhythms, reading widely, trying new things, and laughing lots in between.

We can see from Charlotte's writing that she, too, in the winter of womanhood continued to read deeply, cultivate relationships, and stay intellectually alive. This can happen even amid the busyness of mothering, but it must be intentionally prioritised. The seeds of knowledge can be planted in the heart of any willing mother through mediums such as audiobooks, social media community groups, and free webinar content, even when her hands are seemingly full.

As soon as I started home educating our children, I came alive again with Shakespeare, poetry, Chaucer, classical music, and fables; not out of a requirement to complete an assignment or sit an exam, but for pure enjoyment and growth. I read to inspire my children, laying out delights through books and experiences that stimulated their minds and engaged their interest. However, in all the study to teach them, I had to remind myself to prepare for my contentment as much as I prepared for their content.

I remember hearing the advice of a seasoned homeschooler early on in my home-educating career. They told me that I just had to stay a few days ahead of my children's learning to succeed. Practically this makes sense: if you're walking your child through a math lesson that you're unsure of, get ahead and learn the lesson a few days before you plan to do it with the child and you'll enter the lesson confidently. Whilst I agree with this sentiment and know that lesson planning can be of benefit to our children, I've learnt that to truly grasp the heart behind Charlotte's guidance, we must also embrace a continuous learning journey for ourselves; it's so much more than "winging it" the night before.

As a home educator I can easily find myself returning to late-night lesson planning sessions or cramming a reading in before teaching the next day. But the sweet spot is found when we start to see our personal learning journey as a source of inspiration for our children's education. The degree to which we feed our own minds will impact the learning experience of our children. The one who learns for her own pleasure can ultimately be the one who helps others find pleasure in learning.

Mothers Who Are Inspired by Wisdom

I love to surround myself with creative, intelligent people, not because I'm a snob but because it's widely known that eventually you become a little bit like the people you spend the most time with. If I want to learn to cook better, I don't just read a cookbook—I visit my friend Kyle. She feeds me mouthwatering concoctions whilst I hang out at her kitchen island and watch her wizardly culinary ways. There are those who challenge me to read out of my comfort zone. If I want to know what to read next, I ask a friend as opposed to just googling it. I love my companions and what I regularly learn from them.

There's an ancient proverb in the Bible that advises us to "walk with the wise and become wise; associate with fools and get in trouble."[1] I love this proverb and have taught it to my children, declaring it many times, especially in the midst of raising teenagers. I try to apply it to the friendships and mentors I give a voice to in my life. We grow as much by those around us as by what we put in us.

I have always been struck by this oft-quoted T. S. Eliot poetic warning: "Where is the wisdom we have lost in knowledge? Where is the knowledge we have lost in information?"[2] This old adage seems more relevant than ever in a time when the more information we have, the more it seems to lead to a depletion of wisdom. It is interesting that in the internet age of options, we look to personal testimony and customer reviews as a means of finding a way through. We seek the opinion and perspective of another to help validate or shape our viewpoint. This is why the people we have around us are so important. They influence and shape us more than we realise.

I've spoken to many mothers over the years who have struggled to find like-minded, kindred spirits to walk this journey of lifelong learning with. I believe part of the problem with "bosom buddy" hunting is that our ideals are too high and we have all our expectations wrapped up in one ideal person. Over my years of mothering and home education, I have found friendship, solace, laughter, and comfort from a whole host of women—never just one. I have made the most treasured friends by transitioning relationships from Instagram to Voxer to sitting at the same kitchen counter in Nashville over tears and tacos. Being around women of wisdom is the heart of staying intellectually alive.

With the wonders of modern technology, we don't have to seek wisdom from only those we have the privilege of knowing in real life. I remember hearing Christine Caine, speaker and activist, once talk about seeking wisdom from role models. She said there can often be a reason why you're drawn to someone you don't know in person. There is a purpose to feeling inspired by them and "following" their lives more than others. The desire to draw closer may be there because there's something in them that is either like you or holds the possibility of you becoming like them. I have taken time to examine the speakers, leaders, educators, and writers I feel compelled to follow and often wonder, What is the wisdom in them I am seeking?

Being inspired is very different from being wooed. We are wooed every day by picture-perfect social media images, filters, and snapshot fictional lives. We are naturally attracted to images of life, smiles, colour, and beauty. Many voices will warn us of the terrors of comparison, but if we expect a twinge of it now and again, we can learn to flex that muscle to get over it, move on and, if anything, just appreciate the art. Being inspired by role models can really open us up to new possibilities and perspectives. Strangers may impart to us a rhythm of life, a book recommendation, a room design, or a recipe; whatever it is, true inspiration leads us away from comparison and towards applying wisdom for our own context.

Mothers Who Water Their Own Gardens

My parents recently entrusted the watering of their garden to me whilst they took a trip to the South of England during an English August heat wave. I loved the simplicity of being responsible for a short-term garden project and carried out my hosepipe chores dutifully. As I was circling the outskirts of their garden, I noticed a small, turquoise, hand-decorated wooden bench that I hadn't taken much notice of before. As my eyes traced the beautiful stenciling of a bee's shape, I suddenly recognised my mother's handwriting in the corner. She had scribed a garden poem entitled "Dreams Come True" and, at the end, used the tag *Patricia's Poems*. This simple act of creativity made me smile, but it also drew me to consider again her love of lifelong learning. I have seen her demonstrate her signature learning style, not just on this scribbled garden bench but in every aspect of her life.

My mother is a reader, but not necessarily of Shakespeare, Homer, or Tolstoy; she reads to lean into her creativity and curiosity. I have watched as she reads poetry, biographies, and classic tales of love, turmoil, and intrigue. She takes classes to learn new handcraft skills and encourages others to do so as well. She supports artists and small businesses by buying their crafts and displaying them with pride in her home. She makes, bakes, writes, and creates. And yet she has never been to university, never written a dissertation, never sat through an academic lecture. When I look at her bench, and look at her life, I can see she is fully and most definitely intellectually alive. Just as I have watched my mother over many years, I am reminded that my children are watching me. I am always challenged by what they will uncover about me.

Charlotte's message of mastering intellectual vitality inspires me to develop curiosity, hunger, and the spirit of investigation. For me, this is often done in small bites that keep me eager for more. Each paragraph read, poem heard, or masterpiece viewed will sow another seed of curiosity. Just as we daily serve up the feast of education in our children's lives, so can we cultivate the discipline to allow ourselves time and space to engage our minds with higher thinking. The more we do it, just a few minutes a day, the more we'll grow in interest and the capacity to consume more. We need only read short excerpts from *Anna Karenina*, hear a section of Hamlet's soliloquy, walk briefly down a virtual gallery in Tate Britain, or take a minute to be captivated by a picture of Monet's water lilies. Magical moments of mother learning take us on a journey of connection with thinkers and creators.

We are not engaging with thought and creativity to merely become better teachers; we're engaging because we, too, are born persons, worthy of input, enrichment, and fascination. We can add to the dialogue, lean into new possibilities, and continue our learning journey way beyond our children's learning years.

Being intellectually alive is an attitude of mind, an intentional practice that looks very different for every mother in each season of raising and teaching children. As we know, one of the most-quoted Charlotte Mason mantras is "Let the mother go out to play!" Although Charlotte was never a mother herself, she closely observed families of all kinds during her years in education. She saw the daily pressures on parents, the challenges of work-life balance, and the never-ending list of expectations put upon the Victorian woman. Her antidote to these societal constraints was to remind women that they had a soul that needed tending to as much as their tasks.

It can be easy to lose focus on ourselves when we are so focused on others. We never have to feel guilty about investing in our soul, for in doing so we are overflowing into others as a result. In cultivating wonder, wisdom, rest, and play, we share a bountiful life full of fascinating things with our children. We are sowing into the noble calling of motherhood, enriching our ever-stretched mind and keeping our inner lives malleable. Just as I found the poem on my mother's garden bench, we wait for our children to discover what we have seen and done; they take note of our example and will be inspired for their future. In keeping our minds alive, we leave our signature mark on the world.

TAKE A MASON MOMENT:
Suggestions for Cultivating Intellectual Vitality

- Keep a poetry compilation open and accessible in the kitchen, bathroom, or another room you spend a lot of time in! Whenever you see it, read a poem for just two minutes.
- Join or start a book club. This doesn't have to be extravagant or fancy. Find a small group of women to read along with you. Meet in real life or online to discuss what you enjoyed, disliked, or were inspired by.
- Grab yourself a simple week-to-view diary and jot down nature observations from your kitchen window every day. Note the weather, which birds you saw, and any seasonal changes. Nature journaling is about your observations, not fine art!
- Go for a walk in nature, alone.
- Keep a few books on the go at the same time; a challenging one, an inspiring one, and a delight-filled one. When you get a moment to read, see which one you feel like. Don't forget that audiobooks and Kindle count too!
- Find a like-minded friend to discuss your intellectual thoughts and findings with; even if it's online, you'll be refreshed from processing with someone else.

- Take a solo trip to an art gallery.
- Keep a growth journal with quotes, poems, and titles of music and art or great conversations with friends that have inspired you or helped you grow.
- Listen to a BBC Radio channel or Classic FM whilst you're cooking, cleaning, in the car, or just in the background of your day. You'll pick up on interesting topics of conversation and composers you haven't heard before.
- Go and see a concert, a play, or hear poetry read live; there's nothing like it, and you can often catch them free outdoors in the summer months in many cities across the world.

Chapter 11

Building Kinship
through Community

The wisdom, the experience, the information of each is made profitable for all;
enthusiasm is generated by the union of many for the advance of a cause,
and every member is cheered by the sympathy of his fellow-workers.

E. KITCHING, IN PNEU,
IN MEMORIAM, CHARLOTTE M. MASON

A revolutionary idea just stays an idea unless it's carried forward by
the power of community. The Parents' National Educational Union
(PNEU) was the original transportation system that carried Charlotte
Mason's ideas around the world; but much richer than an institution
or a formal establishment, these ideas were lived out amongst kindred
spirits, mutual motherhood, and sisters in arms. And so too today, we
must find ourselves a kindred community to help us walk together
as we progress forward together into the future.

Finding Fellow Travel Companions

In the quirky 1980s Steve Martin film called *The Lonely Guy* there's a
scene where Steve Martin's character, Larry, walks into a large, busy,
formal restaurant and asks for a table. The host asks for how many,
and Larry says, "I'm alone." At that point the chatter in the restaurant
comes to a dramatic pause, and every person turns to stare at him.
The maître d' then walks the character over to a table whilst a theatre

spotlight embarrassingly follows across the restaurant, shining brightly on him the whole way, until he says thank you and "Please, could everybody go back to talking?"

We have all felt like Larry the lonely guy at points in our lives. Isolation can be confusing and crippling; we tell ourselves that everyone is looking at us, whilst also feeling unnoticed and unknown. Just like Larry, the character of Fanny in Jane Austen's *Mansfield Park* recognised a deep sense of unease that we might be able to relate to in our social media–driven lives:

> Every body around her was gay and busy, prosperous and important, each had their object of interest, their part, their dress, their favourite scene, their friends and confederates, all were finding employment in consultations and comparisons, or diversion in the playful conceits they suggested. She alone was sad and insignificant; she had no share in any thing; she might go or stay, she might be in the midst of their noise, or retreat from it to the solitude of the East room, without being seen or missed.[1]

Comparison with others can be a breeding ground for loneliness, and choosing to educate differently can sometimes leave us feeling set apart from others. It may seem that we are the only ones whose work is insignificant whilst everyone else is basking in their success. But when it feels like no one can relate to you or see you, the antidote is not to surround yourself with more people but rather to find kinship: a sense of shared origin and intimate connection with those who become your fellow travel companions in life. No matter how much you may feel alone even reading this book, I can guarantee that someone out there has felt that pain, fought that battle, suffered that situation, and certainly cried those same tears. Kinship is possible for you.

The use of the word *community* has radically changed over the years, and our ideas about what it looks like has evolved with the rise of social media platforms. The sons and daughters currently being raised in our homes have always been digital natives. To them there is almost no distinction between online and offline friendships, and this is often the same for us. Whilst our experience of community may commonly begin within the squares of Instagram or via an inspiring conversation on an online forum, I am always grateful when these virtual friendships turn seamlessly into in-person relationships that can be cultivated over tea and cake in a National Trust café or around dinner tables brimming with spouses, children, and conversation.

I love being part of a group of people my husband calls my "Mason friends." Community comes to us in small groups or large gatherings; it is the place of connection where we can find people who complement our journey, without having to default to comparison, caricature, conformity, copying, or compliance. Finding a community with fellow Charlotte Mason educators isn't always easy, especially if you are more of an introvert type. Whether online or in person, it can be a terrifying prospect to let people see the real, unfiltered version of us. Yet this is vital for us to thrive as mothers and educators.

A Movement That Was Born from Community

Perhaps the real reason community must be kept at the heart of our Charlotte Mason education is because that is how it began in the first place. The late 1880s brought along a spiritual awakening of types, a Christian revival where churches were growing, Sunday school numbers were increasing, and church leaders were raising resources to send parishioners out on global missions. To help out these endeavours and after seeing the need for parents to grow in their sense of responsibility for the nurturing and education of their children, Charlotte studied for, prepared, and delivered eight lectures in Bradford, West Yorkshire.

These lectures became *Home Education*, the first of the six volumes in the beloved Home Education series.

Charlotte Mason's brave step into the world of educational theory was welcomed and revered. The *Reading Mercury* newspaper at the time commented that she "availed herself of the rich harvest of thought and experience of the past but has, by the way, gleaned new grain and fresh flowers for her readers."[2] The Parents' National Educational Union (PNEU) was formed in 1890, not without its struggles, but poignantly out of relationship, collaboration, an appreciation for Mason's reforming work, and a shared feeling of urgency to equip and enable others to outwork these ideas in their homes. The PNEU, alongside the *Parents' Review* magazine, was an instrument to outwork new ideas in homes and schoolrooms.

Charlotte created a correspondence curriculum first known as the Parents' Review School where the price was considerably less than private school fees. The curriculum was gladly received—cultivating further success. This led her to recognise the importance of training those who would deliver the curriculum, mainly governesses. She launched a training programme at Scale How (her school in Ambleside in the Lake District). Once you start to train the trainers, you begin to see a movement emerge.

The evolving development of the PNEU was the river in which Charlotte's ideas flowed; but like all moving water, it changed its course, collected, and deposited components along the way, ultimately opening a vast ocean of new possibilities for our children and their education. Now in the twenty-first century, we sail on the wide-open space of her ideas, whilst having access to the history of the river's course. As I've read, studied, and looked back at this revolution, I can appreciate the rich depths of the past, but ultimately, we are responsible for keeping this vessel moving. As Charlotte herself said at the 1894 PNEU

Annual General Meeting (AGM): "We are progressive. We take what former thinkers have left us and go on from there."[3]

Today we are those who still stand on the shoulders of giants. The work and impact of the PNEU helps us to see the power of collaboration and the pioneering of a movement within a community that eventually touched the world. Nevertheless, it is not the past that matters but what we do today that counts. As my "Mason friend" Em says, "We are the new PNEU; this community of modern mothers sharing book ideas and ways to implement living ideas is how a philosophy grows in impact." You and I are part of a growing global movement; the nurturing work you are doing every day with your children and in your home will ultimately have a generational impact. The communities you're forming, the conversations you're having, and the books you're discussing are shaping who you are as an educator as well as trickling down into the hearts and minds of others.

A Movement That Still Expands Today

I've had the privilege of interviewing (for the *Modern Miss Mason* podcast) mothers who started home educating their children in the 1980s. These were formative years for bringing Charlotte Mason's ideas and methods back into the forefront of educators' minds, especially in the United States (although there was also a small movement happening in the UK, too). These incredible women formed programmes, republished books, pioneered email lists, blogged about their personal experiences, and produced resources to lighten the load. They held long discussions via Yahoo boards, hosted book clubs, began conferences, and dreamed about trips to the UK to visit Ambleside and Charlotte's archives. Charlotte's legacy was being rekindled through a community that continues to grow today. These early discussions and formations of a new outworking of home education (and within private schools) in the late twentieth and early twenty-first century have been pivotal in children's and families' lives.

Decades on, there are many groups who discuss and learn from Charlotte's ideas. Admittedly, some may not always see eye to eye, but they are mostly connected by the shared foundation that children are born whole persons and ready to interact with the world and words around them, which we can provide. None of this would have been fostered apart from the context of community.

In May 2013 I attended and presented at my first home education conference, here in the UK. I was well established as a home educator, had been reading Charlotte Mason's work for a few years, and was finally finding my feet and freedom. A fellow home educator, Rebecca, and I ran a short workshop together to help others understand what we were learning. We brought along all the books in our collections and from our aching shelves, including nature displays, examples of work, and a whole lot of enthusiasm.

We gathered probably no more than twenty people in a small conference room at a place called Nettle Hill in Warwickshire. We proceeded to pour out everything we knew, had practised, and were passionate about to one another. It felt great to process with like-minded parents and those wanting to sojourn with us. At the end of the session, I threw a piece of paper on a table, with a pen, and said, "If anyone is interested in starting a UK Facebook community, pop your email address down here and we'll set it up." I came home with twelve names, and that summer as we were all gearing up for a new academic year of teaching our children from home, we started "Charlotte Mason Conversations, UK."

Today we have thousands of UK families represented in that online community alone; we've taken our familiar kindred conversations beyond the walls of social media and made lifelong friends. We've gathered in fields and parks with picnics, and a few years ago we began our annual pilgrimage to Ambleside in the Lake District to bond over historic archives, copious cups of tea, and long walks in the Cumbrian hills. These gatherings have broken the boundaries of purism, personal beliefs, and parenting styles and found a common bond through believing that, just maybe, "the souls of all children are waiting for the call of knowledge to awaken them to delightful living."[4] We've opened our doors wide, shown grace, grown together, learnt lessons together, patiently guided one another, and stayed the course as students of the philosophy and as mothers and sisters in arms.

Through the UK gatherings and online conversations, we have taken up the challenge to light a fire in our hearts and continue loving and nurturing our children. Contrary to those who may try to minimise the authenticity and validity of online communities, these places are a true expression of kindred hearts and minds, full of women who can connect and commune daily. They are ideal for those who live in remote areas where in-real-life gatherings are difficult to reach. These spaces are important and help us to stay progressive. In the context of a vibrant community, we can answer the call to take what former thinkers have left us and go on from there.

A Movement That Connects Us with Each Other

As the years have gone by and social media platforms have exploded beyond the blogs, I've been able to share my story and connect with mothers all over the world who are, like me, finding their freedom within this educational philosophy. Although our homeschooling experiences are individual and unique, I don't believe they are meant to be worked out alone. Two minds are always better than one.

Each individual parent carries the responsibility of outworking these ideas with their children, but setting themselves up to do so alongside others in community brings definition and longevity to their mission. I've seen so many messages of exhaustion and confusion posted on our community wall, messages sharing that a mother is about ready to give up. I've been moved by the speed of the online gathering to encourage, share feelings of solidarity, yet begin to nudge her on with ideas, inspiration, and courage. I don't always know or see the true outcome of these interactions—none of us do—but I hope they spur the mother-educator on for another day and hold her for the future.

Community allows us to create a pool of thought, experience, and resources from every type of family. There are families represented in many Mason communities from across the world, of all colours of skin, various languages, all faiths or none; we welcome these shared experiences and voices to beautifully add to our own. We all go away and do our own work, but we're never alone.

I've held many coaching conversations with mothers over the years. My message to anyone who I coach or have the privilege of sharing with via stage or page is that they can find their own freedom within Charlotte's philosophy. I've seen too many mothers try to fit themselves into an education model that is completely foreign to their family culture, especially their children. They become frustrated and exhausted and burn out fast. I wholeheartedly encourage and share ideas with others, but after the tears and inspiration of a shared conversation, each mother must walk those moments out, day by day, in their own way. We focus on our own family, children, and culture, and outwork the philosophy in accordance with that. But it's important to remember that this individuality doesn't have to lead to an isolated experience. It matters not that we do the same thing as others or even agree on everything together. What matters is that we are in it together, cheering one another on towards our unique goals for our unique children.

A Movement That Shares Common Resources
One of the most powerful components of outworking Charlotte's ideas in community is the ability to share ideas around living books and resources. Sure, we can spend hours on a search engine, sifting through

Goodreads reviews, or scouring our friends' bookshelves, but a simple question like "What living book did you guys use for eighteenth century British history?" is usually answered by a whole host of suggestions, detailed reviews, and recommendations based on age level. This living feedback loop is gold dust for the home educator and a lifeline I could not live without. Even though we browse the bookcases of everyone's home, we can ask and engage with our community. Most of the books my family have used over the years have come from the minds and shelves of the UK Mason community—I sincerely couldn't have done my education journey without them.

Community isn't just about what we can gain and learn; it's also a place where we can share our gifts, skills, and ideas as part of remaining intellectually alive. My friend Dr. Carroll Smith of the Charlotte Mason Institute is a huge proponent of mothers sharing and speaking out what they've learnt. We've discussed this together on many occasions. His encouragement is to give out from what you have, no matter how early on you are in your personal learning journey, as your lived experience gives a voice and courage to so many more. I remember being about seven years into my homeschooling journey, having not read all six volumes or fully outworked all Charlotte's ideas, jumping onto the new live video platform Periscope and saying, "Let's find our freedom within this philosophy." I created these regular videos whilst my toddler and baby were napping and my older children were resting, and they were the beginnings of me learning how to teach others to let go of high ideals and to gently work with their children rather than exhaustedly aiming for perfection. When was the last time you bravely shared your voice for the benefit of others?

A Movement That Helps Shape Our Educational Practice

Since the resurgence and growing popularity of Charlotte's philosophy amongst home educators in the USA in the early 1980s, her ideas, methods, and legacy have taken their place in homes and small private schoolrooms across the globe. The PNEU programmes, timetables, and booklists have inspired the creation of many modern curriculums used by home educators all over the world today. Some educators attempt to use the programmes taken straight from the PNEU archives and search deep and wide for the vintage books. Others have recreated and revised the booklists, and many take their inspiration from the foundation of the philosophy and craft their own bespoke curriculum for their children. However archaic some of the programmes look to us today, it is without doubt that they were formed with great skill and intention. And they are the "roots and trunks" that many educators, at home and overseas, take their inspiration from and apply to the culture and setting they are working within.

The PNEU held broad principles which Margaret Coombs describes in her Charlotte Mason biography as "open to variable local interpretation."[5] I personally don't believe we have to directly copy a programme from the past, but I have respect for those who manage to do this if it is right for their family. I do think, however, there are three universal principles found in the PNEU programmes that are helpful for us as we curate our own curriculum for our context.

First, we can see that the Charlotte Mason approach provides a rich and varied education. From the late 1800s right through to the PNEU programmes formed in the 1970s, the suggested lesson format and resources include well-researched living books, age-appropriate application, and plenty of time outdoors. Whether we follow an organised programme or form the daily guides ourselves, we can all appreciate and apply this liberal education for all! In addition, Charlotte advocated keeping lessons short, varied, and interesting so that they did not overwhelm the child and instead brought delight. This is reflected in the programmes over the years.

Second, we see from the PNEU programmes that valuing the

child's age and stage is important. Children follow a pattern of progression from the age of six until the older teen years. Although on paper these suggestions seem rigid and detailed, there is freedom within the format. We must remember that connection and character trump curriculum every time; as we become more and more observant of the born persons within our care, we will instinctively know when to move on and how. As twenty-first-century homeschoolers we're not trying to recreate a Victorian schoolroom or an upper-class, governess-led "nursery," we're facilitating our children's education in a modern era where their needs and futures look very different from those of children living in the 1900s.

Third, it is clear from Mason's PNEU programmes that collaboration with others is key. These programmes were researched and prepared by a myriad of people with academic accolades, teaching expertise, and experience with children. Our Facebook groups and Instagram platforms may look a bit like this today. Don't be afraid to ask for reviews and suggestions or offer your own tried and tested page-turners that your children are reading. Ask and seek far and wide; let's keep our selections and bookcases diverse. Recall the biblical proverb I mentioned in the previous chapter: "Walk with the wise and become wise."[6] I make it a personal mission to befriend fellow students of Charlotte Mason, readers, creatives, and attentive explorers. They make the best of friends and become comrades in arms. If the proverb is true, as we journey and collaborate, we become a little more alike.

A Movement of Individuals, Together

Some friendships are for a reason, and a season, but not always for life. As I've got older, I've homed in on what I look for in community and companionship. I no longer look to find it all in one person as I may have as a younger woman—rather, I seek a collective gathering of women companions. We don't always have to think the same way to be able to connect with each other in kinship.

Charlotte had many friends and colleagues who fitted into the facets of her life and needs. She travelled, worked, rested, and sadly dealt with a constant health battle, but all with companions by her side. Her quiet but assertive manner wooed the hearts of educators and parents alike. But there were a few who appreciated her for so much more than what she could do for them. I want to highlight three particular friends who walked closely with Charlotte, three ladies who have stood out to me over the years as I've read letters, reports, and biographies. I think we can learn so much from the qualities in these women and the friendships they held. It is comforting to know that in a world that so often judges our popularity by the number of online followers we have, it is the quality of our companions that really counts. Let me introduce you to Lienie, Netta, and Kit Kit.

Lienie—a friend who stands by your side

Emeline Steinthal was a wife, mother, and artist who was captivated by Charlotte's writing in *Home Education* and who wrote to her, forming the beginnings of a unique friendship. Lienie found in Charlotte a true mentor and friend. This new confidant was known to be compassionate, kind, and one who always saw the best in other people. Lienie had a concern for the poor, and she gathered children who may have usually been overlooked or forgotten for Sunday school; she taught and showed care, often changing the trajectory of their lives. After many years of the PNEU practices and programmes being used across schools and homes around the world, Lienie pioneered the first trial into a mining village school in Yorkshire where this kind of approach to education was quite foreign. Her efforts were a success, and Charlotte praised her work and had great hope for the future of the philosophy being outworked in all spheres of life.

I've always warmed to Lienie's artistic temperament and creative approach to life; I'm sure she was an incredibly attentive mother, and she leaned on Charlotte as a child does to a loving teacher. But more than this I'm inspired by her commitment to work hard, do whatever it takes, and stand in to lead when Charlotte was sick or travelling. We all need a friend like Lienie. We need people like this in our life who will stand by us when the going gets tough.

Netta—a friend who shares your vision

Henrietta Franklin, a young Liberal Jew, came into Charlotte's life after the PNEU was established, but she came with an upper-class experience of mothering children, a powerful confidence and business acumen, and an abundance of resources to offer the growing establishment. Netta and Charlotte affectionately referred to each other as their "chela"[7]; they complemented and strengthened each other, especially at a time when the foundations of the PNEU were being questioned. Henrietta Franklin was responsible for integrating PNEU principles into schools, as opposed to leaving it merely as an educational tool and programme for parents. Netta and Charlotte's friendship wasn't always easy, and their letters of correspondence over the years reveal this, but what we do see is their unfaltering commitment to children and their shared mission to revolutionise the approach and application of children's education. They may not have shared a similar personality, but they certainly shared a common vision. We all need a friend like Netta—someone who sharpens and shapes who we are. She brought strength and religious diversity to the growing group of education enthusiasts. Her persuasive and managerial skills were much to be desired and admired, adding a fresh dimension to Charlotte's work that gave voice to ideas that otherwise may have taken longer to spread further.

Kit Kit—a friend who has your back

Elsie Kitching was a bright and accomplished daughter of a friend of Charlotte. Elsie had done well academically and was established and well trained in social etiquette and was also acquainted with Charlotte's way of life. Elsie was at a turning point in her life and unsure what to do, when Charlotte suggested she come to live and work with her at Scale How. Affectionately known as Kit Kit, Elsie became Charlotte's right-hand woman, and "her self-effacing vigilance guarded Miss Mason literally day and night, year in, year out."[8] Elsie worked closely with the students, knew the comings and goings of Scale How, was a local nature enthusiast (helping to teach this subject), and saw to Charlotte's every need. In her biography of Charlotte Mason, Margaret Coombs describes Elsie Kitching as one who "unobtrusively served Miss Mason as attentive companion and devoted scribe."[9]

Even in her death Elsie wanted to humbly serve her friend and leader. I've stood many times on what I thought was a plain stone slab in the St. Mary's churchyard to visit Charlotte's gravestone and honour her work. It wasn't until I read Coombs's biography that I realised I'd been standing on Elsie Kitching's unassuming gravestone above where she was interred. This was placed by her request, to continue to be of service to those who wished to visit and honour Charlotte.

On my next visit to Ambleside, I was ready to visit the graveside again, but this time I stood on the grass beside Elsie's slab to honour the significant part both their voices continue to play in my life today. I finally noticed the grey stone engraved with a simple E. K. at the foot of Charlotte's final resting place, with a "K" in every corner.

If it wasn't for the unshakable support of women like Elsie Kitching, I'm not sure Charlotte Mason would have been able to serve the cause of education like she did. We all need a friend like Kit Kit to stand their ground with us, stand up for us, and even sometimes pave the way for us to fulfil the destiny of the born persons we are meant to be.

At the end of the day, we are not meant to walk this journey of life alone. We all need our own versions of Lienie, Netta, and Kit Kit in our lives. I have found mine. We each need to decide to be a friend who stands by the side of others, one who champions the vision of fellow mothers, and the kind of person who loyally fights in the corner of all. It is impossible to walk the challenging road of educating our children until we deal with the desperation of isolation. Whilst we must overcome loneliness in ourselves, we must proactively eliminate it for others, too. Like the placement of Kit Kit's gravestone to make room for others to discover Charlotte, there are times when we humbly reposition our hearts to help other mothers thrive without the fear of being overshadowed. In our gallant efforts to raise children, facilitate their education, and continue to stay strong on our path of identity, we'd do well to invite others along with us. Community can be intimidating and lift us clean out of our well-established comfort zone; but to learn from others, to sense true companionship, and to find those we can grow alongside is worth taking the risk.

TAKE A MASON MOMENT:
Suggestions for Cultivating Community

- If you can't find a community, form a community. If you want to make a friend, then be a friend to someone today.
- Where you can, take a local online connection into real life. Conversation over coffee generally trumps daily direct message trails! The next best things are video calls and voice messages.
- Read a book with a friend.
- Be selective about who you follow, listen to, and align yourself with. Mixed messages can be overbearing and distracting. Avoid the comparison game.

- If you've got a local Charlotte Mason educator friend, try coming together for a shared learning experience. Call it a "club" if you want to take the pressure off having to be the perfect host! We've done nature study, science, and even mathematics with other families, and we've all benefitted from it greatly.
- Open your living room and share your story. Take the risk and share your life with someone you trust.
- Collaborate with others to share your tried and tested ideas and practices.
- Organise a mother's outing, a shared meal in someone's garden, a picnic, or a gathering for coffee and cake. These events can bring a nervous or new mum into friendships that enrich their homeschooling experience, reminding them they are not alone. You can overcome awkwardness as you open your lives to each other.
- Share your skills—if you're no good at handcrafts, find a friend who is; if you're a budding biologist, gather a family or two to learn from you. Don't keep your talents hidden!
- Send letters, postcards, and books to friends in your online communities. Anything that takes an online connection into real homes and hands is worth the work. Stock up on stamps and put a smile on a few friends' faces!
- If you're building a community of influence online, find your authentic following. Collaborate and post online to celebrate, to support, or to ask a question; avoid striving for mentions or entertaining for attention.

Chapter 12

Leaving a Legacy

*The question is not,—how much does the youth know? when he has finished
his education—but how much does he care? and about how many orders
of things does he care? In fact, how large is the room in which he finds
his feet set? and, therefore, how full is the life he has before him?*

CHARLOTTE MASON, *SCHOOL EDUCATION*

*History is made to be built upon, not ignored or disregarded, but to
be heard and honoured whilst leaving us free to herald in the future.
We all have a part to play in marking out a path for our children's
future and the future of the Charlotte Mason philosophy itself.
Every expression of family, individuality, and creativity
expands on the living legacy that Charlotte lived and
worked out for us, reimagined in our unique way.*

Nothing Ever Gets Left Behind

One day Charlotte was talking to her friend Elsie Kitching, and she
uttered these memorable words . . . "I do not wish my life to be written, it is the work that matters: it will live."[1] As much as Charlotte
didn't want to become a household name herself, it was important to
her that the work lived on; that a legacy of learning would be left in
all children's lives. We can see from the story arc of her life and work,

especially through her many books on education, that no experience
or moment of revelation was ever wasted. All that she learnt she used
to lay a stronger foundation for those of us taking up her mantle today.

During a recent visit to Ambleside, I was privileged to have a guided
tour around Scale How, Charlotte's House of Education, and some of
the rooms surrounding it. I was already in awe of the opportunity to
walk the staircases Charlotte did all those years ago; as I slid my hand
up the Georgian wooden banister, I wondered how many times a day
she'd graced these same steps and stared out of the window from the
top of the stairs onto the tree-lined courtyard. As the building manager walked me around the back of the House of Education, he casu-
ally said, "Have you heard the story of the Millet Room?" to which I
answered (wide-eyed and eager to hear), "No, do tell!" I'd obviously
skimmed past the slight mentions of this story in the two biographies
I'd read about Charlotte Mason, but on returning home I eagerly got
to work to discover the story in detail.

At the back of Scale How there's a room marked with a carved
stone that says "Millet." The artist Fred Yates had been asked to give
a talk to Charlotte Mason's trainee governesses during an Ambleside
visit. He was a confident and experienced lecturer on the works of
Jean-François Millet, and as he didn't come to Ambleside equipped
with reproductions or a slideshow, he merely went ahead and drew
with charcoal on the walls of the handicrafts room,[2] stating, "What
a lovely surface. Charcoal will easily rub off." Charlotte, however,
"insisted that the drawings should be fixed to preserve them for students to come."[3]

Nine of the reproductions that Yates drew that day are still on
the walls of what is now a university building.[4] As I slowly lingered
and looked at Yates's charcoaled copies of Millet's *The Sower* and
Washerwomen with the oral retelling from the building manager ring-
ing in my ears, I was again overwhelmed with gratitude.

I was in awe of the privilege of seeing history preserved on the walls and captured again by Charlotte's ability to take something so simple and make sure it had a legacy. Little did she know that one day a home-school mum from Yorkshire would read her work, be unequivocally impacted, teach her own children at home a hundred years after her death, and share her story with the world. But here we all are.

Not all is lost or wiped away by the passing of time.

Growing in Our Vision

If we are going to leave a legacy for our children, then we need to be clear on why we are doing what we are doing in the first place. One of the things we need to overcome as homeschooling mothers is the voice of the inner inspector. Traditional schools may have an inspection sprung upon them every few years to check up on the attainment and outcomes of pupils. But the challenges for the homeschooler are that they don't just have an external inspection occasionally—they can live with their own inner inspector that makes judgements on their level of success every single day! The voice of the inner inspector may sound like a disapproving family member who wonders why your child is not in real school. It may echo a friend who just doesn't get what you do with your time all day. It can reflect the myriad of expert voices who are pulling you in a thousand different directions that all point to how you are not doing it right. But worst of all, the inner inspector can sound like our own anxious fears that come knocking without notice. We fear failure, fear we are not doing enough, and fear it won't work for us when we don't see immediate results.

All we have to do is read a few letters from the "postbag" section of an early 1900s *Parents' Review*, and we are reminded that parents are parents, no matter what century or year it is. Mothers have the same worries, the same questions about book choices, and the same in-house conversations about whether they are getting it right or not!

The only way we can hope to overcome this crippling inner voice of judgement is by reminding ourselves about the vision of why we came into homeschooling in the first place. Some people got on this path as a reaction against a school system they felt failed them. It wasn't really a choice but a necessity. Others were lured by a romanticised dream of being at home with their children, only to find it is tougher than it looks. However you started this journey and for whatever reasons—whether difficult, naive, or bold—it is vital you stop right now and reassess why you are doing what you are doing if you are going to make it for the long haul. You must have a clear vision and a compelling reason for educating your child at home that acts like an anchor when the storms inevitably come.

Clarity of vision helps us see beyond the challenges of the daily grind and gives us hope for a brighter tomorrow. So why do you do what you do? What are the benefits and the outcomes you really want? Is it about growing in your connection with your children? Is it about creating a shared journey of beautiful learning? Is it about academic success whilst preparing your children for the modern world? Is it about giving them the kind of enriching opportunities you never had yourself?

Maybe it is about all these things and more. Taking time to consider the big picture of what you want from home education allows you to effectively guard against inner fear or external judgement and can also provide a way to make your own framework by which to measure success. If you set out to spend more loving, quality time with your children and you have ended up more stressed and frayed than ever, then it may be time to make some adjustments. A compelling *why* acts as a plumb line to help you stay level when things get shaken.

Growing in Our Convictions

Once we are clear on our vision, then it's equally important that we are clear on our non-negotiables, too. Susan Schaeffer Macaulay notes in *When Children Love to Learn* that missionary Amy Carmichael had to interpret Charlotte's books for her Indian missionary context by focusing on the root of the thinking:

> The Ambleside books by her on education were sent out
> to India to Amy Carmichael, who founded the Dohnavur
> Fellowship. She too recognised in the writings the "roots
> and trunk" she was looking for as she cared for and educated
> Indian children.[5]

As we shape our own "roots and trunks," we endeavour to teach our children valuable lessons from history, whether it's from inspirational stories or from troubled and tragic situations from the past—yet here we are, living very much in the present day. A famous saying of mine from the beginning of my time writing and sharing about home education was "I'm not aiming to recreate a Victorian classroom in my home." And I don't think Charlotte Mason ever intended her successors (you and I) to recreate her methods, subject lists, ways of physically exercising, or even the exact books she used. If she's the woman we think she was—progressive, visionary, up to date on research in her area of work, and more importantly, humble—I'm of the opinion that she'd be cheering us on in experimenting with fresh ideas, creatively collaborating with others, and making modern application of her teachings.

Whilst there are some who are genuinely interested in the historical methods of the PNEU (whether sloyd, drill, or Plutarch), we need to keep moving forward into the future. There's nothing wrong with implementing traditional lessons that have been reshared on a blog or social media platform, but it can appear to those in the early years phase that this is something that *must* be implemented to "fully do" a Charlotte Mason education. I've tried to avoid being prescriptive, especially in my later years as I began to understand that it's the core roots and trunks of her ideas that will cultivate freedom, not a preloaded curriculum.

Charlotte Mason laid out many principles based on her years of experience with children and families; she was also well read, well connected, and well acquainted with the need for educational reform. Her principles shaped how most school days looked within the PNEU; they are printed at the beginning of all her six volumes of work, and they continue to be referred to by commentators today. But she didn't expect these principles to stay set in stone. On this topic she said, "The fact is, that a few broad essential principles cover the whole field, and these once fully laid hold of, it is as easy and natural to act upon them as it is to act upon our knowledge of such facts as that fire burns and water flows."[6]

Karen Glass, in her book *In Vital Harmony*, reminds us that "principles should result in action."[7] It matters not what we believe but what we do as a result that counts. To find our own nonnegotiable roots and trunks, we must answer two key questions: "What do you believe about children, and what do you believe about education?" If we can begin with a wide view on a connected education and the belief that children are born with everything they need to search for and assimilate that knowledge, then we are off to a strong start.

Modern Miss Mason was never about pushing a personal agenda. I began to share my family's educational story on social media and created places for other families to share theirs, and the term *Modern Miss Mason* emerged within the comments on live videos! I decided to take the name and use it to find kindred spirits around the world; I wanted to create a place where every face fits within the Charlotte Mason philosophy. Every family is so unique, overflowing with individual needs, experiences, and available resources—the last thing any of us needs is another barrier. I regularly remind parents that they are the experts on their children, and no matter how underqualified they feel in comparison to others, the fact is no one knows their children like they do.

I recently spent the day with a friend at her intriguing Derbyshire farmhouse; Victoria described how this beautifully large, old property had a fake wall built up around the original brickwork, making it look more modern than it was. Inside the house were original beams and fireplaces, giving a more authentic feel to the property. But the interior didn't match the exterior. This can happen in our homeschooling, too. We can build up the scaffolding of modern formulas, systems, and curriculums that seemingly create safety and convenience, but it can hide the heart of what can really make a difference in our lives and the lives of our children. The reason why it doesn't produce freedom is because we have decorated the exterior rather than dealing with the interior. A modern approach tears down the fake walls and gets back to the roots. This is not always about the methods, but it is always about the people.

The twenty-first-century expression of Charlotte's philosophy is a refreshing way to view childhood, motherhood, and education, and it's an invitation with a huge welcome sign at the door. Part of our continued work is to create a place and platform so that everyone can experience our support and hospitality. We are invited to come and share our story, adding our voice to the growing sound of parents and children finding their freedom to search the world for knowledge that finally connects with who they are and who they were born to be. This is a movement not just for the elite or special. The idea that the philosophy is too overwhelming or "highbrow" and academic is one that needs to be quashed. How does this approach authentically reflect your family values, the skills and experience you have, and the resources available to you?

Growing in Our Mindset

If we are going to keep going for the long term, then continual growth, not fixed outcomes, must become the goal for all education. The concept of continual growth must remain at the heart of our homeschool journey or else we fall into the danger of becoming stuck and stagnated in our efforts. In words from Charlotte's time, we must keep moving forward to stay effective and sharp: "But, if we would do our best for our children, grow we must; and on our power of growth surely depends, not only our future happiness, but our future usefulness."[8]

According to well-known educational research by Dr. Carol Dweck, there are two types of mindset that fundamentally affect our lives in either a positive or negative way.[9] A *fixed mindset* is when people believe their basic abilities are static traits that cannot be enhanced. A person with a fixed mindset spends their time proving, measuring, or complaining about their existing talents instead of putting in the effort to develop them. Yet in a *growth mindset*, people believe that their most basic abilities can be developed through dedication and hard work. Raw talent is just the starting point. The seeds are all there, but they still need to be watered. It is clear from Charlotte's philosophy that this idea of developing a mindset for growth is foundational to her idea of lifelong learning. She always saw growth as the goal of education, citing ideas such as this: "We must bear in mind that *growth*, physical, intellectual, moral, spiritual, is the sole end of education"[10] or phrases such as "The function of education is not to give technical skill but to develop a person."[11]

The way in which children think about and reflect on their own learning can have a significant long-term effect on their progress. A growth mindset is just as important to grasp for the educator as it is for the student. Unless the parent becomes a resilient educator, we will never see resilient children. We need to think realistically about the time and effort it will take to learn. Don't expect to become a master overnight, and don't ask that of your children straight away. Help them see where they are on the journey. What is the next step for them or you? Learning fast isn't the same as learning well. Value growth over speed.

There are four keys to developing a growth mindset that can help us as we seek to keep going for the long haul. The first way we can grow either as educators or learners is to try something new. Trying new things can open amazing opportunities. Growth-minded people learn how to constantly create new goals and find new opportunities to keep themselves stimulated. It helps people engage with subjects and activities that they may otherwise try to avoid through fear of getting things wrong or "not being good enough." There's no one-size-fits-all model for learning. What works for one person may not work for another. Be prepared to adapt and take a different approach. If at first you don't succeed, change your angle of approach!

The second way we can encourage growth is to raise our expectations. It is commonly believed that lowering our expectations promotes better self-esteem in children ("Never mind, let's try an easier one"), but this is not the case. Having high expectations shows that you believe they can do it, which in turn has a positive impact on their own beliefs, behaviours, and outcomes. When we set high expectations, we can offer critique and feedback as a means of growth, not personal criticism. Feedback is our friend when given in the context of a loving, nurturing relationship. If we value progress over perfection, we will enjoy the learning process even when it continues beyond an expected time frame. Teach children to try to tackle big things by using the edible elephant analogy. How do you eat an elephant? One bite at a time!

The third way we grow is when we accept that we will probably make mistakes. According to someone with a fixed mindset, if you fail at something, or even need to put effort in, it must be because

"You're just not good enough." Because of that belief, children begin to avoid challenges and choose activities that they find easy. Hiding from weaknesses means you'll never overcome them. Find a group of people that you feel safe to explore, expand, and learn with. Making mistakes with people you trust will make it easier to take risks in the future. Failure is an opportunity to grow, not the limit of your abilities. We must learn to fail better and continually ask ourselves, "What can I do better next time?"

The fourth way we grow is by learning to use the language of resilience to promote growth. Charlotte had a well-known empowering motto she used with children: "I am, I ought, I can, I will."[12] Although this is interpreted in often wildly different ways across the Charlotte Mason community, these words are based on Longfellow's "Ladder of St. Augustine," which is fundamentally about rising above to reach a higher place of growth than where we are now. Don't rush to let children say "I can't" but rather introduce the word *yet* into their vocabulary. Remind children they just don't know it *yet* or can't do it *yet*. Remind them of their favourite athlete, musician, or artist, and talk about their journey to success. Rather than focusing on somebody's natural talents, focus on the effort they put in to get where they are now by unlocking their God-given potential. May our children rise to their best as we create the environment for continual growth in every season.

Growing in Our Gratitude

I've often wondered what I'd say to Charlotte if I came face to face with her today! What element of her life and teaching would I start with and thank her for? Mothers have been humbly thanking Charlotte for her work since the late 1800s; the boxes and boxes of moving letters stored in the archives at the Armitt Museum in Ambleside show this time and time again.

I recently spent hours sifting through piles of letters from Charlotte's archives. The letters were sent from mothers and educators all over the country, and eventually the world, communicating words of praise and gratitude for her work. One letter in particular stood out to me, written in 1887, from Mary L. Hart Davis in Reading.

> I do not know if this letter will ever reach you, and should
> it do so you will find that I am a total stranger to you, but I
> owe you so much gratitude for your book "Home Education"
> that I have long felt I must some day try to thank you for it. I
> know of the book through a notice in the *Spectator* and got it
> early in this past most beautiful summertime. I have read and
> reread it so many times, that much of it is a possession for
> life, and I can most truly say that it has given me inspiration,
> strength of purpose, guidance and courage which has made a
> real difference to me in health.[13]

Charlotte faithfully replied, as she always did, with a sincere and heartfelt note reiterating that Mrs. Hart Davis was doing a wonderful job, that her work was worthy, and that she should believe herself to be a teacher of great value and status. My hope is that you and I might find the same "inspiration, strength of purpose, guidance and courage." May we receive the encouragement today that our work is worthy.

I have walked for some time with Charlotte Mason; her life and educational legacy have framed my understanding of childhood, education, and motherhood, and I'm forever grateful for the threads of inspiration woven throughout the days and years as I've raised and led my children and lived my very full life. Discovering her ideas opened a wide door of opportunity, making room for my own innovation and creativity rather than tying me down to formality. This approach to education isn't restrictive or oppressive, rather it's a liberating movement giving you freedom to explore the world and its creators, authors, and thinkers, past and present, alongside your children, from birth to graduation!

Charlotte wanted her work to be known, not her name; yet fortunately for us the two were never separated. Now the legacy lives on in you and me. The seeds of thought and inspiration that have danced through your mind as you've moved through these pages now need to be planted and watered. And when we put these ideas into practice, the legacy will live on in our children, too.

At the time of writing this book, my children are still building towards their own future. My eldest, Nyah, has just graduated from formal secondary school with distinctions in science and is entering the world of health and social care, possibly considering joining the emergency medical services. My son Joel is loving his hands-on apprenticeship, where he is training to be an electrician and enter a trade. My third child, Micah, is probably somewhere in the house creating another wonderfully written animated story for his YouTube channel. And my youngest, Sienna, is likely practicing her singing lessons whilst plotting to change the world! Though their paths, interests, focus, and even careers may change, their foundation will not. I am learning to focus on the long-term outworkings and not just the short-term outcomes.

Leading a Charlotte Mason inspired life does not automatically ensure high academic achievement, guarantee career outcomes, or produce uniform, conforming adults. Giving freedom for our children and young adults to live a rich life served from a varied platter of thought, inspiration, and creativity will allow them to live out their born person lives in the light of it all. I long to live in a world where electricians know Shakespeare and add care and conversation to the lives of their colleagues, clients, and work; where paramedics hear Kipling's words when faced with tragedy and know they can keep their head when others all about them are losing theirs. I want to see the work of designers, illustrators, and animators presenting stories of heroes, history, and hope. I long to hear the sound from singers and actors on twenty-first-century stages inspired by the soundtrack of their child-hood, still hearing their mothers' voices filling the atmosphere with music that lifted people's spirits, spoke to them of salvation, or simply brought peace into the core of their home.

We must keep going. And we must keep growing—for the children's sake.

It's time to reimagine what the legacy will look like, together.

Dear Charlotte

MAY 5, 2021
AMBLESIDE, LAKE DISTRICT

There were celandines on Kit Kit's gravestone today.
Dandelions on yours.
A seeming reflection of how we've come to know you:
Choosing to see and celebrate the beauty in others,
Whilst you linger where seeds disperse
And longevity becomes deeply rooted.

That's why I'm here.
Along with many others.
Mothers moving the work on,
Tilling the soil,
And reaping the reward.

I read the inscription, again.
"She devoted her life to the work of education."
I felt my lips mouth out the words.

Today, I'm carrying wildflower seeds in my pocket.

I dug dirt with my hands,
And sprinkled small, sand-like grains into the soil
In the gap, by your grave.
I raked with my fingers,
And then the rain came,
As I drove away from Ambleside.

Maybe you'll enjoy aster, cornflower, or yarrow this summer.
Or maybe the seed will settle and wait?
I'm sure you'd grade this as glory.
Because good things grow slow,
Go down deep,
And reproduce.

Dear Charlotte, may your legacy live on
In the lives of those who sow.

Acknowledgements

Many describe the life of a writer as being a lonely one. Sure, there were times I sat on my own to write—at my desk, in coffee shops, and at the table in a beautiful barn conversion in Ullswater, Lake District (ever grateful to you, Victoria; Thornythwaite Farm is a gift)—but I was never alone on this journey. After I signed with Punchline Agency, my literary agent, Joy, encouraged me to "take the Modern Miss Mason community along with you on the journey," and it was some of the best advice an agent could ever give. Yes, it has felt like the longest wait to get this book actually in your hands, but you have truly held mine and walked with me every step of the way. Some of us met in the early days of my naptime Periscope videos or on the squares of Instagram. For others, we shared a meal in Sicily, took a rainy nature walk in Cumbria, made our way through a pot of tea in my Coventry kitchen, or waved to each other from a stage in California. For all of you, I see you, and the stories you have shared are etched on my heart.

I wish I could type every one of your names out for the world to see, and the names of every precious child you are raising, but alas, I cannot. So here lies my small effort to truly say thank you to the Modern Miss Mason community, in all its shapes and forms. These names represent all of you. Thank you, Annie Williamson, Joanne Bodell, Leanne Beardsley, Maritza Duranti, Hannah Kewley, Maria Louise Peters, Jo Downing, Olumfunmike Alabi, Bernadette Magsalin-Manuel, Marie Yo, Rita M. Gleason, Rachel Dye, Tiffany Devens, Sarah Szalkowski, Kelly Rosenbalm, Olivia E. Weaver, Angela DeMatteo, Savannah Kentzell, Sarah Rose LaBrie, Jessica Chou, Eleanor Le Mesurier, L. J. Warwick, Nida Tariq, Rachel McGimsey, Pippa Pain, Julie Cerdas, Antonia Braithwaite, Anya Anderson, Polly Smith, Jessica Quinn Telian, Sara Lee Fouts, Amii Ruan, and Angelué Hamilton.

The *Modern Miss Mason* story is ever entwined with the global work of Wild + Free. Ainsley Arment not only generously wrote the foreword for this book, but she gave this English mama an opportunity to share on the page and on the stage of the Wild + Free community. Thank you, dear friend.

Greta, that bleary-eyed post-conference breakfast date with you in Franklin's Frothy Monkey was divinely ordained. Rachel, you and Dan are two of the kindest, most generous people I know. Thank you for creatively processing my Wild + Free writing ideas and bringing them to life with your beautiful photography. Amy, I'm sorry I didn't write a whole chapter about you as you'd hoped, but I "ate that frog" and wrote a book, and I know you will too. Andi and Hilda, you are dear friends, and gracious, sweet hosts. Our Nashville adventures together in nature, in estate sales, and in bookstores mark an important chapter in my life. Thank you.

To my grassroots homeschool community, the CHEW and CMC UK groups who have been consistent and present, no matter how much I have been able to engage or not: thank you from the bottom of my heart, Juliet English, Victoria Beech, Laura Thiessen, Alice Khimasia, Hilary Sephton, Em Bowers, Holly Kindness, and Emily Haigh.

Hilary, thank you for championing my crazy ideas over coffee in my kitchen, being a consistent, peaceful presence in my life, and for keeping me grounded, whether you realised it or not!

A huge thank you to Faye and her team at The Armitt Museum in Ambleside; your hospitality and that welcome cup of tea as I sifted through boxes of Charlotte's letters and archives formed a beautiful and important part of my book-writing memories.

I want to thank the leadership and community of Mosaic Church and particularly our Pastors Gary and Helen Spicer. Despite Gary insisting on calling what I do "home tutoring" for the duration of the decade we worked together, he and Helen never failed to support me, pray for me, and speak encouragingly over my endeavours. Dave and I love you both dearly.

Thank you to Gav, Viv, Don, Heidi, Scott, Naomi, Mark, and Beccy for asking good questions, showing interest in my niche work, and praying for me through the process. Every time you asked about "the book," it meant the world to me.

To Diana, Christine, Kat, Em, and Gemma, my CMC UK team: ladies—I'm sorry for all the times I abandoned my post due to being in the depths of this book. Thank you for all your hard work, support, and commitment to building a beautiful Charlotte Mason community in the UK and Ireland.

Holly Eagle, Hannah Haigh, Anna Symonds, and Amy McGlynn: this book is written for you and your precious children. Every writer is encouraged to have an audience avatar—a face and life they are writing for; I had four. You draw out of me what God has put in—keep asking questions, loving your children, and seeking first God's Kingdom.

Serena McCarthy, from your book recommendations to our Friday breakfasts and all the years we built before, you are my treasured friend. Thanks for helping me think and feel. Kyle Campbell, your joy and tenacity knows no bounds; you have listened to my ideas, processed at length with me, dreamed with me, and prayed those dreams into being. Thank you for breathing love, care, inspiration, and ridiculous amounts of creativity into my life. Lynn Seddon, thank you for believing in me, listening to me, encouraging me, praying for me, and for being a shining light in the Charlotte Mason community since the early days. You are a dear friend. Lucy Joy Wilman, your friendship and our shared laughter is a constant source of delight to me. Thanks for assuming we'll do a book tour together and for carefully considering what we'll wear. Let's share tea, tears, and treats together, forever. And thank you, my dear Dr. Mary Louder, who always knew I had it in me. Your encouragement, mentoring, and friendship over the years have been and continue to be a balm to my soul.

To my family, Mum and Dad, your names are the legacy that is littered throughout this book. Thank you for all you have sown and continue to sow into my life. An incredible legacy of faith, love, and beauty from the beginning. Beth, your beauty sense and creative spark are an enormous inspiration to me. Jonathan, your entrepreneurial spirit and boundless joy are a fuel for anyone, especially me. To all the Sheffields, Bodens, Blakes, and Joneses—I love you. Thank you for cheering me on and asking all the important questions about the launch party!

To my agent, Joy, and the incredible team at Tyndale Momentum— thank you for the opportunity, skill, and expertise you have shared, enabling us to breathe this book into being.

My whole heart and gratitude for Dave, Nyah, Joel, Micah, and Sienna-Raine. I'm so proud of all of you; I'm truly the richest woman in the world with you in my life.

To all the Charlotte Mason–inspired parents, writers, bloggers, academics, researchers, and leaders who have done the work, run ahead, and cleared the way—thank you.

For Charlotte and for the children's sake.

Soli Deo Gloria

Notes

INTRODUCTION: WALKING WITH CHARLOTTE

1. Brené Brown, *Dare to Lead: Brave Work. Tough Conversations. Whole Hearts.* (London: Vermilion, 2018), 215.
2. Andrea da Firenze, *The Triumph of Saint Thomas Aquinas*, 1368, fresco, Spanish Chapel at Santa Maria Novella, Florence, Italy.
3. Julia Child, Louisette Bertholle, and Simone Beck, *Mastering the Art of French Cooking* (New York: Knopf, 1961).
4. Susan Schaeffer Macaulay, "The Value of Charlotte Mason's Work for Today," in *When Children Love to Learn: A Practical Application of Charlotte Mason's Philosophy for Today*, ed. Elaine Cooper (Wheaton, IL: Crossway Books, 2004), 25.
5. Anas Atassi, "Food, Family, Friends," *Simple Things*, June 23, 2021, PressReader, https://www.pressreader.com/uk/the-simple-things/20210623/282364042620722.
6. Reem Kassis, "Do You Have Nafas, the Elusive Gift That Makes Food Taste Better?" *New York Times*, April 1, 2021, https://www.nytimes.com/2021/04/01/dining/nafas-makes-food-taste-better.html.

CHAPTER 1 RAISING HUMANS

1. Charlotte Mason's 1st principle from her 20 principles. Charlotte M. Mason, short synopsis in *An Essay towards a Philosophy of Education: A Liberal Education for All* (London: Kegan Paul, Trench, Trubner, 1925).
2. Charlotte Mason's 4th principle from her 20 principles. Mason, short synopsis in *Philosophy of Education*.
3. Mason, *Philosophy of Education*. "A liberal education for all" is the subtitle of the book.

4. Charlotte M. Mason, *Home Education*, rev. ed. (London: Kegan Paul, Trench, Trubner, 1906), 43.

5. Charlotte Mason's 2nd principle from her 20 principles. Mason, short synopsis in *Philosophy of Education*.

6. Stacia Tauscher, quoted in Deborah DeFord, Judy Speicher, and Mark LaFlaur, eds., *"Quotable" Quotes: Wit & Wisdom for Every Occasion* (Pleasantville, NY: Reader's Digest Association, 1997), 57.

7. Susan Schaeffer Macaulay, *For the Children's Sake: Foundations of Education for Home and School* (Wheaton, IL: Crossway Books, 1984), 12.

CHAPTER 2 LAYING FOUNDATIONS

1. Charlotte M. Mason, *Parents and Children*, rev. ed. (London: Kegan Paul, Trench, Trubner, 1904), 32, 248.

2. Charlotte M. Mason, *An Essay towards a Philosophy of Education: A Liberal Education for All* (London: Kegan Paul, Trench, Trubner, 1925), 96.

3. Mason, *Philosophy of Education*, 96.

4. BJ Fogg, *Tiny Habits: The Small Changes That Change Everything* (Boston: Houghton Mifflin Harcourt, 2020), 19–20.

5. See Proverbs 22:6.

6. Charlotte M. Mason, *Home Education*, rev. ed. (London: Kegan Paul, Trench, Trubner, 1906), 137.

7. Mason, *Philosophy of Education*, 261.

8. Charlotte Mason's 13th principle from her 20 principles. Mason, short synopsis in *Philosophy of Education*.

9. This is a recurring theme in Mason, *Philosophy of Education*.

CHAPTER 3 CAPTURING ATTENTION

1. Charlotte M. Mason, *Home Education*, rev. ed. (London: Kegan Paul, Trench, Trubner, 1906), 146.

2. Mason, *Home Education*, 69.

3. Mason, *Home Education*, 140.

4. Mason, *Home Education*, 230.

5. John Medina, *Brain Rules: 12 Principles for Surviving and Thriving at Work, Home, and School*, rev. ed. (Seattle: Pear Press, 2014), 123.

6. Medina, *Brain Rules*, 119.

7. Simon Jenkins, "Covid Has Shown That England's Schools Are Desperate for Reform," *Guardian*, February 19, 2021, https://www.theguardian.com/commentisfree/2021/feb/19/covid-england-schools-reform-nhs-exams.

8. For more on learning styles, see "Vak Test: What Is Your Visual, Auditory, and Kinesthetic Type?" ProProfs, last updated October 26, 2021, https://www.proprofs.com/quiz-school/story.php?title=vak-quiz-visual-auditory-kinesthetic.

CHAPTER 4 STANDING BACK

1. Charlotte M. Mason, *School Education* (London: Kegan Paul, Trench, Trubner, 1905), chap. 3.
2. Mason, *School Education*, 30.
3. David F. Lancy, *Raising Children: Surprising Insights from Other Cultures* (Cambridge: Cambridge University Press, 2017), 1–2.
4. Ellen Beate Hansen Sandseter and Ole Johan Sando, "'We Don't Allow Children to Climb Trees': How a Focus on Safety Affects Norwegian Children's Play in Early-Childhood Education and Care Settings," *American Journal of Play* 8, no. 2 (January 2016): 178–200.
5. Jenny King, *Charlotte Mason Reviewed: A Philosophy of Education* (Devon: Stockwell, 1981), 29.
6. Charlotte M. Mason, *An Essay towards a Philosophy of Education: A Liberal Education for All* (London: Kegan Paul, Trench, Trubner, 1925), 240.
7. Mason, *School Education*, 29.

CHAPTER 5 MASTERS OF NARRATION

1. Charlotte M. Mason, *Home Education*, rev. ed. (London: Kegan Paul, Trench, Trubner, 1906), 231.
2. See, for example, "The Learning Pyramid," Education Corner, accessed February 23, 2022, https://www.educationcorner.com/the-learning-pyramid.html.
3. Mason, *Home Education*, 231.
4. Charlotte M. Mason, *School Education* (London: Kegan Paul, Trench, Trubner, 1905), 177.
5. Charlotte M. Mason, *An Essay towards A Philosophy of Education: A Liberal Education for All* (London: Kegan Paul, Trench, Trubner, 1925), 20.
6. Mason, *Home Education*, 96.

CHAPTER 6 TREASURERS OF LIVING BOOKS

1. Charlotte M. Mason, *Self-Direction*, in *Ourselves*, rev. ed. (London: Kegan Paul, Trench, Trubner, 1905), bk. 2, 11.
2. Charlotte M. Mason, *School Education* (London: Kegan Paul, Trench, Trubner, 1905), 82–83.
3. Mason, *Self-Direction*, in *Ourselves*, 11.
4. Mason, *Self-Direction*, in *Ourselves*, 10.
5. Mason, *Self-Direction*, in *Ourselves*, 10.
6. Mason, *School Education*, 177.
7. Mason, *School Education*, 178.
8. Emily Style, "Curriculum as Window and Mirror," National SEED Project, originally published in *Listening for All Voices* (1988), https://nationalseedproject.org/Key-SEED-Texts/curriculum-as-window-and-mirror.

9. Amber O'Neal Johnston, foreword to *Gladiola Garden*, by Effie Lee Newsome (Living Book Press, 2020; Associated Publishers, 1944).

10. Melanie Ramdarshan Bold, *Representation of People of Colour among Children's Book Authors and Illustrators* (London: BookTrust, April 2019), https://www.booktrust.org.uk/globalassets/resources/represents/booktrust-represents-diversity-childrens-authors-illustrators-report.pdf.

11. "Baroness Floella Benjamin: 'Being a Playschool Presenter Was an Opportunity to Change the World,'" interview by Justin Johnson, BFI, video, 14.59, https://www.youtube.com/watch?v=xBitqUG-TVs.

12. Floella Benjamin, "My Latest Book," Floella Benjamin's official website, accessed February 25, 2022, http://www.floellabenjamin.com/my-latest-book/.

13. Mason, *Self-Direction*, in *Ourselves*, 9.

14. Charlotte M. Mason, *Home Education*, rev. ed. (London: Kegan Paul, Trench, Trubner, 1906), see especially page 229.

15. Kylea Suman, "The Book Trust Key Three: Key 1: Choice," March 20, 2017, BookTrust, https://www.booktrust.org/blog/book-trust-key-three-key-1-choice/.

16. Charlotte M. Mason, *An Essay towards A Philosophy of Education: A Liberated Education for All* (London: Kegan Paul, Trench, Trubner, 1925), xxv.

17. Mason, *Philosophy of Education*, xxv.

CHAPTER 7 EXPLORERS OF NATURE STUDY

1. Charlotte M. Mason, *Home Education*, rev. ed. (London: Kegan Paul, Trench, Trubner, 1906), 43–44.

2. "'Let Nature Be Your Teacher,'" New Forest National Park Authority, April 21, 2020, https://www.newforestnpa.gov.uk/blog/let-nature-be-your-teacher/.

3. Mason, *Home Education*, 63.

4. William Wordsworth, "The Lesser Celandine," lines 1–4.

5. Julie Fowlis et al., "The Lost Words Blessing" (2019), line 11, The Bird Sings, https://thebirdsings.com/lost-words-blessing/.

CHAPTER 8 INVESTORS IN CULTURAL CAPITAL

1. E. D. Hirsch Jr., *Cultural Literacy: What Every American Needs to Know*, rev. ed. (New York: Vintage Books, 1988), xiii.

2. Ofsted, *School Inspection Handbook* (UK, 2019), updated February 9, 2022, GOV.UK, https://www.gov.uk/government/publications/school-inspection-handbook-eif/school-inspection-handbook.

3. Essex Cholmondeley, *The Story of Charlotte Mason*, rev. ed. (Cambridge: Lutterworth Press, 2021), 103, 206.

4. Charlotte M. Mason, *Home Education*, rev. ed. (London: Kegan Paul, Trench, Trubner, 1906), 174.

5. Ofsted, *School Inspection Handbook*.

6. *Mona Lisa Smile*, directed by Mike Newell (Columbia Pictures/Revolution Studios, 2003).

7. Charlotte M. Mason, *Self-Knowledge*, in *Ourselves* (London: Kegan Paul, Trench, Trubner, 1905), bk. 1, chap. 5.

8. Mason, *Self-Knowledge*, in *Ourselves*, 43.

9. Susanna Clarke, *Piranesi* (New York: Bloomsbury, 2020), 243.

10. Clemency Burton-Hill (@Clemencybh), Instagram, https://www.instagram.com /p/CKc7cTxgNPB/, January 25, 2021.

11. Linda Semple (@lindafsemple), May 22, 2021, comment on Clemency Burton-Hill, "This 90-year-old legend is releasing his latest book," May 20, 2021, Instagram, https://www.instagram.com/p/CPHklVjgrzO/.

12. Myriam V. Thoma et al., "The Effect of Music on the Human Stress Response," *PLOS One* 8, no. 8 (2013): e70156, https://www.ncbi.nlm.nih.gov/pmc/articles /PMC3734071/.

13. Mrs. Glover, address, Ambleside Conference of the Parents' Union, 1922, quoted in Charlotte M. Mason, *An Essay towards a Philosophy of Education: A Liberal Education for All* (London: Kegan Paul, Trench, Trubner, 1925), 217.

14. "Who Was This Mysterious Ballerina from the Viral *Swan Lake* video?" *The Current*, CBC Radio, November 16, 2020, https://www.cbc.ca/radio/thecurrent /the-current-for-nov-16-2020-1.5803389/who-was-this-mysterious-ballerina -from-the-viral-swan-lake-video-1.5803747.

CHAPTER 9 CREATING SOUL SPACE

1. Jennifer Wallace, "Why It's Good for Grown-ups to Go Play," *Washington Post*, May 20, 2017, https://www.washingtonpost.com/national/health-science/why -its-good-for-grown-ups-to-go-play/2017/05/19/99810292-fd1f-11e6-8ebe -6e0dbe4f2bca_story.html.

2. See Genesis 26:18.

3. Genesis 26:22, NKJV.

4. Charlotte M. Mason, *Home Education*, rev. ed. (London: Kegan Paul, Trench, Trubner, 1906), 44.

5. Charlotte M. Mason, *School Education* (London: Kegan Paul, Trench, Trubner, 1905), 33–34.

6. Shauna Niequist, *Present over Perfect: Leaving Behind Frantic for a Simpler, More Soulful Way of Living* (Grand Rapids, MI: Zondervan, 2016), 36.

7. Elsie Kitching, as recorded in Parents' National Educational Union, *In Memoriam, Charlotte M. Mason* (London: Parents' National Educational Union, 1923), 71.

8. A., "Mother Culture," *Parents' Review* 3, no. 2 (1892/93): 92–95, AmblesideOnline, https://amblesideonline.org/PR/PR03p092MotherCulture.shtml.

9. Julia Cameron, "Artist Dates," *The Artist's Way*, Julia Cameron's official website, accessed March 2, 2022, https://juliacameronlive.com/basic-tools/artists-dates/.

10. Instagram direct message to author, September 26, 2021.

CHAPTER 10 BECOMING INTELLECTUALLY ALIVE
1. Proverbs 13:20.
2. T. S. Eliot, *The Rock* (Harcourt, Brace, 1934), pt. 1, lines 15–16.

CHAPTER 11 BUILDING KINSHIP THROUGH COMMUNITY
1. Jane Austen, *Mansfield Park* (1814), rev. ed., ed. John Wiltshire (Cambridge: Cambridge University Press, 2005), 187.
2. *Reading Mercury*, January 1, 1887, quoted in Margaret A. Coombs, *Charlotte Mason: Hidden Heritage and Educational Influence* (Cambridge: Lutterworth Press, 2015), 146.
3. Charlotte Mason, quoted in Coombs, *Charlotte Mason: Hidden Heritage*, 183–84.
4. Charlotte M. Mason, preface to *An Essay towards A Philosophy of Education: A Liberal Education for All* (London: Kegan Paul, Trench, Trubner, 1925).
5. Coombs, *Charlotte Mason: Hidden Heritage*, 159.
6. Proverbs 13:20.
7. The pincers on a crab or lobster, used for defense, feeding, or courtship.
8. Coombs, *Charlotte Mason: Hidden Heritage*, 9.
9. Coombs, *Charlotte Mason: Hidden Heritage*, 257.

CHAPTER 12 LEAVING A LEGACY
1. Essex Cholmondeley, editorial in *The Story of Charlotte Mason, 1842–1923*, rev. ed. (Cambridge: Lutterworth Press, 2021).
2. Margaret A. Coombs, *Charlotte Mason: Hidden Heritage and Educational Influence* (Cambridge: Lutterworth Press, 2015), 204.
3. Cholmondeley, *Story of Charlotte Mason*, 74.
4. "Discover the Millet Drawings," University of Cumbria, accessed March 5, 2022, https://www.cumbria.ac.uk/alumni/memory-lane/charlotte-mason-college/archives-and-special-collections/discover-the-millet-drawings/.
5. Susan Schaeffer Macaulay, "The Value of Charlotte Mason's Work for Today," in *When Children Love to Learn: A Practical Application of Charlotte Mason's Philosophy for Today*, ed. Elaine Cooper (Wheaton, IL: Crossway Books, 2004), 25.
6. Charlotte M. Mason, *Home Education*, rev. ed. (London: Kegan Paul, Trench, Trubner, 1906), 10.
7. Karen Glass, *In Vital Harmony: Charlotte Mason and the Natural Laws of Education* (self-pub., 2019), 9.
8. A., "Mother Culture," *Parents' Review* 3, no. 2 (1892/93): 92–95, AmblesideOnline, https://www.amblesideonline.org/PR/PR03p092MotherCulture.shtml.

9. Carol S. Dweck, *Mindset: The New Psychology of Success* (New York: Random House, 2006).

10. Cholmondeley, *Story of Charlotte Mason*, 206.

11. Charlotte M. Mason, *An Essay towards a Philosophy of Education: A Liberal Education for All* (London: Kegan Paul, Trench, Trubner, 1925), 147.

12. Mason, *Philosophy of Education*, 29.

13. Mary L. Hart Davis to Charlotte Mason, 1887, Charlotte Mason archives, The Armitt Museum Gallery and Library, Ambleside, Cumbria, England, https://archive.org/details/PNEU2AFilepneu8/i01p1-i04p11pneu8/mode/2up?q=hart.

About the Author

Leah Boden is wife to Dave, mother to four children, and a long-time home educator. With over two decades of experience in church leadership, Leah's working background also features many years in youth, children's, and family work within the church and for the local education authority. Currently Leah's life and teaching focus on the practice and pedagogy of late nineteenth/early twentieth century educator Charlotte Mason. Leah leads the Charlotte Mason Conversations UK online community as well as being the founder of Modern Miss Mason, an international initiative to help parents and children find their freedom within Charlotte Mason's philosophy. She writes, speaks, hosts podcasts and coaching sessions, and runs workshops sharing the beauty of a Charlotte Mason approach to childhood, motherhood, and education.

Leah, Dave, and their family live in the West Midlands, England, with their rescue dog, Eli. When she's not writing, Leah is drinking tea, reading through her home library, lingering around art, or exploring nature in their local park.